family cooking

family cooking

easy recipes for great meals

This edition specially produced for Netto

© Anness Publishing Ltd 2003

A CIP catalogue record for this book is available from the British Library.

Publisher: Joanna Lorenz
Designers: Tony Paine and Roy Prescott
Jacket Designer: Peter Ridley
Photographers: Karl Adamson, Edward Allright, David Armstrong,
Steve Baxter, James Duncan, Amanda Heywood, Janine Hosegood,
Patrick McLeavey, Michael Michaels, Thomas Odulate
Food for Photography: Carla Capalbo, Kit Chan, Jacqueline Clark,
Joanna Craig, Nicola Fowler, Carole Handslip, Jane Hartshorn, Wendy Lee,
Lucy McKelvie, Annie Nichols, Jane Stevenson, Steven Wheeler and
Elizabeth Wolf Cohen
Props Stylists: Madeleine Brehaut, Maria Kelly, Blake Minton and
Kirsty Rawlings
Additional Recipes: Carla Capalbo, Roz Denny, Rosamund Grant,
Soheila Kimberley, Hilaire Walden and Laura Washburn

1 3 5 7 9 10 8 6 4 2

Notes
For all recipes, quantities are given in both metric and imperial measures and,
where appropriate, measures are also given in standard cups and spoons.
Follow one set, but not a mixture, because they are not interchangeable.

Standard spoon and cup measures are level.
1 tsp = 5ml, 1 tbsp = 15ml, 1 cup = 250ml/8 fl oz

Australian standard tablespoons are 20ml. Australian readers should use 3 tsp in
place of 1 tbsp for measuring small quantities of gelatine, cornflour, salt, etc.

Size 3 (medium) eggs are used unless otherwise stated

FRONT COVER
Tomato or plain risotto (see page 56) can be jazzed up for special occasions by
the addition of prawns, bacon or chicken, with a variety of herbs, spices and
garnishes (as seen on the front cover).

CONTENTS

SOUPS AND STARTERS

The following recipes have been chosen to complement the main courses in this book, ideal for when you are hosting a dinner party or enjoying a special family gathering. The soups, which range from traditional Cock-a-leekie to American-style Prawn and Sweetcorn Chowder, can also be served for lunch or supper with lashings of crusty bread. The delicious starters include family favourites such as Chicken Liver Pâté and Potted Shrimps, together with tasty Hot Tomato and Mozzarella Salad and King Prawns in Crispy Batter.

Carrot and Coriander Soup

Carrot soup is best made with young carrots when they are at their sweetest and tastiest. With older carrots you will have to use more to get the full flavour. This soup freezes well.

INGREDIENTS

Serves 5–6

1 onion, chopped
15ml/1 tbsp sunflower oil
675g/1½lb carrots, chopped
900ml/1½ pint/3¾ cups chicken stock
few sprigs fresh coriander, or 5ml/1 tsp dried
5ml/1 tsp lemon rind
30ml/2 tbsp lemon juice
salt and black pepper
chopped fresh parsley or coriander, to garnish

1 Soften the onion in the oil in a large pan. Add the chopped carrots, the stock, coriander leaves, lemon rind and juice and seasoning to taste.

2 Bring to the boil, cover and simmer for 15–20 minutes, occasionally checking that there is sufficient liquid. When the carrots are really tender, blend or liquidize and return to the pan, then check the seasoning.

3 Heat through again and sprinkle with chopped parsley or coriander before serving.

Prawn and Sweetcorn Chowder

This soup is perfect for informal entertaining as it is quite special but not too extravagant.

INGREDIENTS

Serves 4

15g/½oz/1 tbsp butter
1 onion, chopped
300g/11oz can sweetcorn
30ml/2 tbsp lemon juice
300ml/½ pint/1¼ cups fish or vegetable stock
115g/4oz/1 cup cooked, peeled prawns
300ml/½ pint/1¼ cups milk
15–30ml/1–2 tbsp cream or yogurt
salt and black pepper
4 large prawns in their shells and a few sprigs parsley or dill, to garnish

1 Heat the butter in a pan and cook the onions until translucent. Add half the sweetcorn and all its liquid, the lemon juice, stock and half the prawns.

2 Cover and simmer the soup for about 15 minutes, then blend or liquidize the soup until quite smooth.

3 Return the soup to the pan and add the milk, the rest of the prawns, chopped, and the sweetcorn, the cream or yogurt and seasoning to taste. Cook gently for 5 minutes, or until reduced sufficiently.

4 Serve each portion garnished with a whole prawn and a herb sprig.

Split Pea and Pumpkin Soup

Salt beef is often used in this creamy pea soup.

INGREDIENTS

Serves 4

225g/8oz split peas, soaked
1.2 litres/2 pints/5 cups water
25g/1oz/2 tbsp butter or margarine
1 onion, finely chopped
225g/8oz pumpkin, chopped
3 fresh tomatoes, peeled and chopped
5ml/1 tsp dried tarragon, crushed
15ml/1 tbsp chopped fresh coriander
2.5ml/$\frac{1}{2}$ tsp ground cumin
vegetable stock cube, crumbled
chilli powder, to taste
coriander sprigs, to garnish

1 Soak the split peas overnight in enough water to cover, then drain. Place the split peas in a large saucepan, add the water and boil for about 30 minutes until cooked.

2 In a separate pan, melt the butter or margarine and sauté the onion for a few minutes until soft but not browned.

3 Add the pumpkin, tomatoes, tarragon, coriander, cumin, vegetable stock cube and chilli powder and bring to the boil.

4 Stir the vegetable mixture into the cooked split peas and their liquid. Simmer gently for 20 minutes or until the vegetables are tender. If the soup is too thick, add another 150ml/$\frac{1}{4}$ pint/ $\frac{2}{3}$ cup of water. Serve hot, garnished with coriander.

Spicy Vegetable Soup

INGREDIENTS

Serves 4

½ red onion
175g/6oz each, turnip, sweet potato
  and pumpkin
30ml/2 tbsp butter or margarine
5ml/1 tsp dried marjoram
2.5ml/½ tsp ground ginger
1.5ml/¼ tsp ground cinnamon
15ml/1 tbsp chopped spring onion
1 litre/1¾ pint/4 cups well-flavoured
  vegetable stock
30ml/2 tbsp flaked almonds
1 fresh chilli, seeded and chopped
5ml/1 tsp sugar
25g/1oz creamed coconut
salt and freshly ground black pepper
chopped coriander, to garnish

1 Finely chop the onion, then peel the turnip, sweet potato and pumpkin and chop into medium-size dice.

2 Melt the butter or margarine in a large non-stick saucepan. Fry the onion for 4–5 minutes. Add the diced vegetables and fry for 3–4 minutes.

3 Add the marjoram, ginger, cinnamon, spring onion, salt and pepper. Fry over a low heat for about 10 minutes, stirring frequently.

4 Add the vegetable stock, flaked almonds, chopped chilli and sugar and stir well to mix, then cover and simmer gently for 10–15 minutes until the vegetables are just tender.

5 Grate the creamed coconut into the soup and stir to mix. Sprinkle with chopped coriander, if liked, spoon into warmed bowls and serve.

Cock-a-Leekie

This traditional soup recipe – it is known from as long ago as 1598 – originally included beef as well as chicken. In the past it would have been made from an old cock bird, hence the name.

INGREDIENTS

Serves 4–6
2 chicken portions, about 275g/
   10oz each
1.2 litres/2 pints/5 cups chicken stock
bouquet garni
4 leeks
8–12 prunes, soaked
salt and black pepper
soft buttered rolls, to serve

1 Gently cook the chicken, stock and bouquet garni for 40 minutes.

2 Cut the white part of the leeks into 2.5cm/1in slices and thinly slice a little of the green part.

3 Add the white part of the leeks and the prunes to the saucepan and cook gently for 20 minutes, then add the green part of the leeks and cook for a further 10–15 minutes.

4 Discard the bouquet garni. Remove the chicken from the pan, discard the skin and bones and chop the flesh. Return the chicken to the pan and season the soup. Heat the soup through, then serve hot with soft buttered rolls.

Scotch Broth

Sustaining and warming, Scotch Broth is custom-made for chilly Scottish weather, and makes a delicious winter soup anywhere.

INGREDIENTS

Serves 6–8
1kg/2lb lean neck of lamb, cut into
   large, even-sized chunks
1.75 litres/3 pints/7½ cups water
1 large onion, chopped
50g/2oz/¼ cup pearl barley
bouquet garni
1 large carrot, chopped
1 turnip, chopped
3 leeks, chopped
½ small white cabbage, shredded
salt and black pepper
chopped parsley, to serve

1 Put the lamb and water into a large saucepan and bring to the boil. Skim off the scum, then stir in the onion, barley and bouquet garni.

2 Bring the soup back to the boil, then partly cover the saucepan and simmer gently for 1 hour. Add the remaining vegetables and the seasoning to the pan. Bring to the boil, partly cover again and simmer for about 35 minutes until the vegetables are tender.

3 Remove surplus fat from the top of the soup, then serve hot, sprinkled with chopped parsley.

Hot Tomato and Mozzarella Salad

A quick, easy starter with a Mediterranean flavour. It can be prepared in advance, chilled, then grilled just before serving.

INGREDIENTS

Serves 4

450g/1lb plum tomatoes, sliced
225g/8oz mozzarella cheese, sliced
1 red onion, finely chopped
4–6 pieces sun-dried tomatoes in oil, drained and chopped
60ml/4 tbsp olive oil
5ml/1 tsp red wine vinegar
2.5ml/½ tsp Dijon mustard
60ml/4 tbsp chopped fresh mixed herbs, such as basil, parsley, oregano and chives
salt and black pepper
fresh herb sprigs, to garnish (optional)

1 Arrange the sliced tomatoes and mozzarella in circles in four individual shallow flameproof dishes.

2 Scatter over the chopped onion and sun-dried tomatoes.

3 Whisk together the olive oil, vinegar, mustard, chopped herbs and seasoning. Pour over the salads.

4 Place the salads under a hot grill for 4–5 minutes, until the mozzarella starts to melt. Grind over plenty of black pepper and serve garnished with fresh herb sprigs, if liked.

Asparagus with Tarragon Butter

Eating fresh asparagus with your fingers can be messy, but it is the only proper way to eat it!

INGREDIENTS

Serves 4

500g/1¼lb fresh asparagus
115g/4oz/½ cup butter
30ml/2 tbsp chopped fresh tarragon
15ml/1 tbsp chopped fresh parsley
grated rind of ½ lemon
15ml/1 tbsp lemon juice
salt and black pepper

COOK'S TIP

When buying fresh asparagus, choose spears which are plump and have a good even colour with tightly budded tips.

1 Trim the woody ends from the asparagus spears, then tie them into four equal bundles.

2 Place the bundles of asparagus in a large frying pan with about 2.5cm/1in boiling water. Cover and cook for about 6–8 minutes, until the asparagus is tender but still firm. Drain well and discard the strings.

3 Meanwhile, melt the butter in a small pan. Add the tarragon, parsley, lemon rind and juice and seasoning.

4 Arrange the asparagus spears on four warmed serving plates. Pour the hot tarragon butter over the asparagus and serve at once.

Mushrooms Stuffed with Walnuts and Tomatoes

INGREDIENTS

Serves 4

50g/2oz/½ cup walnuts, roughly
 chopped
4 sun-dried tomatoes in oil, drained
115g/4oz/½ cup soft cheese
12 closed cup mushrooms, about
 225g/8oz, stalks removed
15ml/1 tbsp butter
50g/2oz/½ cup grated Manchego or
 Cheddar cheese
salt and coarsely ground black pepper
flat leaf parsley, to garnish

COOK'S TIP

For a delicious variation, use only half the
filling, coat the mushrooms in flour, egg
and breadcrumbs and deep-fry until crisp.

1 Place the chopped walnuts in a
small frying pan. Shake the pan
over a gentle heat for 3–5 minutes
until the walnuts are golden brown.
Chop the sun-dried tomatoes.

2 Tip the walnuts into a bowl and
stir in the sun-dried tomatoes and
soft cheese, with salt and pepper to
taste. Fill the mushroom caps with
the mixture.

3 Preheat the grill to medium-high.
Melt the butter in a flameproof
dish large enough to hold all the
mushrooms in a single layer. Add the
mushrooms, stuffing-side up, then grill
gently for about 7 minutes.

4 Sprinkle the mushrooms with the
cheese and then grill for 5 minutes
more, until the cheese is bubbling and
the mushrooms are tender. Serve hot,
garnished with flat leaf parsley.

Baked Peppers and Tomatoes

Make sure there is a basket of warm bread on hand so that none of the delicious juices from this dish are wasted.

INGREDIENTS

Serves 8
2 red peppers
2 yellow peppers
1 red onion, sliced
2 garlic cloves, halved
6 plum tomatoes, quartered
50g/2oz/¼ cup black olives
5ml/1 tsp soft light brown sugar
45ml/3 tbsp sherry
3–4 rosemary sprigs
30ml/2 tbsp olive oil
salt and freshly ground black pepper

1 Seed the red and yellow peppers, then cut each into 12 strips.

2 Preheat the oven to 200°C/400°F/ Gas 6. Place the peppers, onion, garlic, tomatoes and olives in a large roasting tin. Sprinkle over the sugar, then pour over the sherry. Season well, cover with foil and bake for 45 minutes.

3 Remove the foil from the tin and stir the mixture well. Add the rosemary sprigs.

——— COOK'S TIP ———

Use four or five well-flavoured beefsteak tomatoes instead of plum tomatoes if you prefer. Cut them into thick wedges instead of quarters.

4 Drizzle over the olive oil. Return the tin to the oven for a further 30 minutes until the vegetables are tender. Serve hot.

Goat's Cheese Tarts

INGREDIENTS

Serves 6

6–8 sheets filo pastry (about
    115g/4oz)
50g/2oz/4 tbsp butter, melted
350g/12oz firm goat's cheese
9 cherry tomatoes, quartered
120ml/4fl oz/½ cup milk
2 eggs
30ml/2 tbsp single cream
large pinch of white pepper

COOK'S TIP

Keep the filo pastry under a damp cloth
while working to prevent the sheets from
drying out.

1 First, preheat the oven to 190°C/
375°F/Gas 5.

2 Grease six 10cm/4in tartlet tins.
Then for each tin, cut out four
rounds of filo pastry, each about
11.5cm/4½in in diameter. Place one
round in the tin and brush with butter.
Top with another filo round and
continue until there are four layers of
filo; do not butter the last layer. Repeat
for the remaining tins.

3 Place the pastry-lined tins on a
baking sheet. Cut the goat's cheese
log into six slices and place a slice of
cheese in each of the pastry cases.

4 Arrange the tomato quarters
around the goat's cheese slices.

5 Place the milk, eggs, cream and
pepper in a measuring jug or bowl
and whisk to mix. Pour into the pastry
cases, filling them almost to the top.

6 Bake in the oven for 30–40
minutes, until puffed and golden.
Serve hot or warm, with a mixed
green salad if desired.

Baked Eggs with Tarragon

Traditional *cocotte* dishes or small ramekins can be used, as either will take one egg perfectly.

INGREDIENTS

Serves 4
40g/1½oz/3 tbsp butter
120ml/4fl oz/½ cup double cream
15–30ml/1–2 tbsp chopped fresh
   tarragon
4 eggs
salt and black pepper
fresh tarragon sprigs, to garnish

1 Preheat the oven to 180°C/350°F/ Gas 4. Lightly butter four small ovenproof dishes, then warm them in the oven for a few minutes.

2 Meanwhile, gently warm the cream. Sprinkle some tarragon into each dish, then spoon in a little of the cream.

3 Carefully break an egg into each of the prepared ovenproof dishes, season the eggs with salt and pepper and spoon a little more of the cream over each of the eggs.

4 Add a knob of butter to each dish and place them in a roasting tin containing sufficient water to come halfway up the sides of the dishes. Bake for 8–10 minutes, until the whites are just set and the yolks still soft. Serve hot, garnished with tarragon sprigs.

Fried Potatoes with Aïoli

Aïoli is a Catalan speciality which began life as a mixture of garlic, salt and olive oil, pounded together with a pestle in a mortar. Nowadays, it is usually made in a food processor and is more like garlic mayonnaise.

INGREDIENTS

Serves 4
4 potatoes, cut into 8 wedges each
vegetable oil, for deep frying
coarse sea salt

For the aïoli
1 large egg yolk, at room
 temperature
5ml/1 tsp white wine vinegar
75ml/5 tbsp olive oil
75ml/5 tbsp sunflower oil
4 garlic cloves, crushed

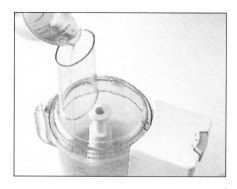

1 Make the aïoli. Place the egg yolk and vinegar in a food processor. With the motor running, add the olive oil, about 10ml/2 tsp at a time.

2 When all the olive oil has been added, add the sunflower oil in the same way, until the aïoli resembles a thick mayonnaise. If it is too thick, add a little more vinegar. Stir in the garlic and salt to taste. Cover and chill.

3 Heat the oil in a saucepan until a cube of bread turns golden in 60 seconds. Add the potatoes and cook for 7 minutes until pale golden.

4 Remove the potato wedges from the pan and drain on kitchen paper. Raise the heat of the oil slightly – it should be hot enough to brown a cube of bread in 30 seconds. Return the potatoes to the pan and cook for 2–3 minutes until golden brown. Drain on kitchen paper and sprinkle with salt. Serve hot with the aïoli.

--- COOK'S TIP ---

This aïoli recipe has equal quantities of olive oil and sunflower oil, but aïoli can be made with 3 parts sunflower oil to 1 part olive oil for a milder flavour. If made solely with olive oil, the finished aïoli will have a waxy appearance and strong, slightly bitter flavour.

King Prawns in Crispy Batter

Serve with an oriental-style dipping sauce or offer a simple tomato sauce or lemon wedges.

INGREDIENTS

Serves 4

120ml/4fl oz/½ cup water
1 size 2 egg
115g/4oz/1 cup plain flour
5ml/1 tsp cayenne pepper
12 raw king prawns, in the shell
vegetable oil, for deep frying
lemon wedge and flat leaf parsley,
   to garnish

For the dipping sauce

30ml/2 tbsp soy sauce
30ml/2 tbsp dry sherry
10ml/2 tsp clear honey

1 In a large bowl, whisk the water with the egg. Add the flour and cayenne and whisk until smooth.

2 Carefully peel the prawns, leaving just the tail sections intact. Make a shallow cut down the back of each prawn, then pull out and discard the dark intestinal tract.

3 To make the dipping sauce, stir together the soy sauce, dry sherry and honey in a small bowl.

4 Heat the oil in a large saucepan or deep fryer, until a cube of bread browns in 1 minute.

5 Holding the prawns by their tails, dip them into the batter, one at a time shaking off any excess. Drop the prawns carefully into the oil and fry for 2–3 minutes until crisp and golden brown. Drain on kitchen paper and serve with the dipping sauce, garnished with a lemon wedge and parsley.

COOK'S TIP

If you have any batter left over, use it to coat thin strips of vegetable such as sweet potato, beetroot, carrot or pepper, or use small broccoli florets or whole baby spinach leaves. Deep-fry until golden.

Pears and Stilton

Stilton is the classic British blue cheese, but you could use another flavourful cheese such as blue Cheshire or Gorgonzola.

INGREDIENTS

Serves 4

4 ripe pears, lightly chilled
75g/3oz blue Stilton cheese
50g/2oz medium fat soft cheese
black pepper
watercress sprigs, to garnish

For the dressing

45ml/3 tbsp light olive oil
15ml/1 tbsp lemon juice
10ml/½ tbsp toasted poppy seeds
salt and pepper

1 First make the dressing; place the olive oil, lemon juice, poppy seeds and seasoning in a screw-topped jar and shake together until emulsified.

2 Cut the pears in half lengthways, then scoop out the cores and cut away the calyx from the rounded end.

3 Beat together the Stilton, soft cheese and a little pepper. Divide this mixture among the cavities in the pears.

4 Shake the dressing to mix it again, then spoon it over the pears. Serve garnished with watercress.

Potted Shrimps

The tiny brown shrimps traditionally used for potting are very fiddly to peel. Since they are rare nowadays, it is easier to use peeled, cooked shrimps instead.

INGREDIENTS

Serves 4

225g/8oz shelled shrimps
225g/8oz/1 cup butter
pinch of ground mace
salt
cayenne pepper
dill sprigs, to garnish
lemon wedges and thin slices of brown bread and butter, to serve

1 Chop a quarter of the shrimps. Melt 115g/4oz/½ cup of the butter slowly, carefully skimming off any foam that rises to the surface.

2 Stir all the shrimps, the mace, salt and cayenne into the pan and heat gently without boiling. Pour the shrimps and butter mixture into four individual pots and leave to cool.

3 Heat the remaining butter in a clean small saucepan, then carefully spoon the clear butter over the shrimps, leaving behind the sediment.

4 Leave until the butter is almost set, then place a dill sprig in the centre of each pot. Leave to set completely, then cover and chill.

5 Transfer the shrimps to room temperature 30 minutes before serving with lemon wedges and thin slices of brown bread and butter.

Chicken Liver Pâté

This rich-tasting, smooth pâté will keep in the fridge for 3–4 days. Serve with thick slices of hot toast or warm bread – a rustic olive oil bread such as ciabatta is the ideal choice.

INGREDIENTS

Serves 8

115g/4oz chicken livers, thawed if frozen, trimmed
1 small garlic clove, chopped
15ml/1 tbsp sherry
30ml/2 tbsp brandy
50g/2oz/¼ cup butter, melted
1.5ml/¼ tsp salt
fresh herbs and black peppercorns, to garnish
hot toast and warm bread, to serve

1 Preheat the oven to 150°C/300°F/Gas 2. Place the chicken livers and chopped garlic in a food processor and whizz until smooth.

2 With the motor running, gradually add the sherry, brandy, melted butter and salt.

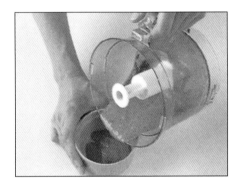

3 Pour the mixture into two 7.5cm/3in ramekins and cover with foil.

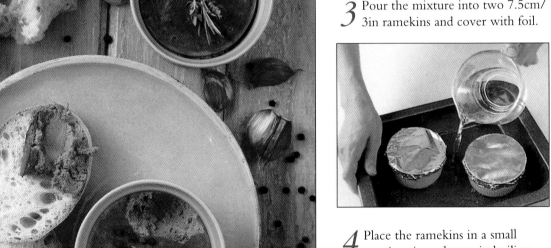

4 Place the ramekins in a small roasting tin and pour in boiling water until it comes halfway up the sides of the ramekins.

5 Carefully transfer the tin to the oven and bake for 20 minutes. Allow to cool to room temperature, then remove the ramekins from the tin and chill until ready to serve. Serve the pâté with toast or bread, garnished with herbs and peppercorns.

Smoked Haddock Pâté

Arbroath smokies are small haddock that are deheaded and gutted but not split before being salted and hot-smoked.

INGREDIENTS

Serves 6

3 large Arbroath smokies, about 225g/
    8oz each
275g/10oz/1¼ cups medium fat soft
    cheese
3 eggs, beaten
30–45ml/2–3 tbsp lemon juice
pepper
sprigs of chervil, to garnish
lemon wedges and lettuce leaves,
    to serve

1 Preheat the oven to 160°C/325°F/
Gas 3. Butter six ramekin dishes.

2 Lay the smokies in a baking dish and heat through in the oven for 10 minutes. Carefully remove the skin and bones from the smokies, then flake the flesh into a bowl.

COOK'S TIP

There should be no need to add salt to this recipe, as smoked haddock is naturally salty – taste the mixture to check.

3 Mash the fish with a fork and work in the cheese, then the eggs. Add lemon juice and pepper to taste.

4 Divide the fish mixture among the ramekins and place in a roasting tin. Pour hot water into the roasting tin to come halfway up the dishes. Bake for 30 minutes, until just set.

5 Allow to cool for 2–3 minutes, then run a knife around each dish and invert on to a warmed plate. Garnish with chervil sprigs and serve with the lemon and lettuce.

MEAT AND POULTRY DISHES

There are a wide selection of main course recipes within this chapter suitable for a variety of meals, from light lunches and suppers through easy mid-week meals to dishes suitable for family celebrations or when entertaining. Some highlights include quick-and-easy Stir-fried Turkey with Mange-tout, the all-round family dish of Sausage and Bean Ragoût, and the classic Chicken Parcels with Herb Butter.

Lamb Pie with a Potato Crust

A pleasant change from meat and potatoes – healthier, too.

INGREDIENTS

Serves 4

750g/1½lb potatoes, diced
30ml/2 tbsp skimmed milk
15ml/1 tbsp wholegrain or French
  mustard
450g/1lb lean minced lamb
1 onion, chopped
2 celery stalks, sliced
2 carrots, diced
150ml/¼ pint/⅔ cup beef stock
60ml/4 tbsp rolled oats
15ml/1 tbsp Worcestershire sauce
30ml/2 tbsp fresh chopped rosemary,
  or 10ml/2 tsp dried
salt and black pepper

1 Cook the potatoes in boiling, lightly salted water until tender. Drain and mash until smooth, then stir in the milk and mustard. Meanwhile, preheat the oven to 200°C/400°F/Gas 6.

2 Break up the lamb with a fork and cook without fat in a non-stick pan until lightly browned. Add the onion, celery, and carrots to the pan and cook for 2–3 minutes, stirring.

3 Stir in the stock and rolled oats. Bring to the boil, then add the Worcestershire sauce and rosemary, and season to taste with salt and pepper.

4 Turn the meat mixture into a 1.8 litre/3 pint/7 cup ovenproof dish and spread over the potato topping evenly, swirling with the edge of a knife. Bake for 30–35 minutes, or until golden. Serve hot with fresh vegetables.

COOK'S TIP

You can prepare this pie up to a day ahead. Cover and chill until ready to bake. Allow the pie to come back to room temperature before baking, or add a few minutes extra cooking time.

Baked Pasta Bolognese

INGREDIENTS

Serves 4

30ml/2 tbsp olive oil
1 onion, chopped
1 garlic clove, crushed
1 carrot, diced
2 celery sticks, chopped
2 rashers streaky bacon, finely chopped
5 button mushrooms, chopped
450g/1lb lean minced beef
120ml/4fl oz/½ cup red wine
15ml/1 tbsp tomato purée
200g/7oz can chopped tomatoes
sprig of fresh thyme
225g/8oz/2 cups dried penne pasta
300ml/½ pint/1¼ cups milk
25g/1oz/2 tbsp butter
25g/1oz/2 tbsp plain flour
150g/5oz/1 cup cubed mozzarella
    cheese
60ml/4 tbsp grated Parmesan cheese
salt and black pepper
fresh basil sprigs, to garnish

1 Heat the oil in a pan and fry the onion, garlic, carrot and celery for 6 minutes, until the onions have softened.

2 Add the bacon and continue frying for 3–4 minutes. Stir in the mushrooms, fry for 2 minutes, then add the beef. Fry on a high heat until well browned all over.

3 Pour in the red wine, the tomato purée dissolved in 45ml/3 tbsp water, and the tomatoes, then add the thyme and season well. Bring to the boil, cover the pan and simmer gently for about 30 minutes.

4 Preheat the oven to 200°C/400°F/ Gas 6. Bring a pan of water to the boil, add a little oil and cook the pasta for 10 minutes.

5 Meanwhile, place the milk, butter and flour in a saucepan, heat gently and whisk continuously with a balloon whisk until thickened. Stir in the mozzarella cheese, 30ml/2 tbsp of the Parmesan and season lightly.

6 Drain the pasta when it is ready and stir into the cheese sauce. Uncover the Bolognese sauce and boil rapidly for 2 minutes to reduce the liquid.

7 Spoon the sauce into an ovenproof dish, top with the pasta mixture and sprinkle the remaining 30ml/2 tbsp Parmesan cheese evenly over the top. Bake for 25 minutes until golden. Garnish with basil and serve hot.

Beef Paprika with Roasted Peppers

This dish is perfect for family suppers – roasting the peppers gives a new dimension.

INGREDIENTS

Serves 4

30ml/2 tbsp olive oil
675g/1½lb chuck steak, cut into
   4cm/1½in cubes
2 onions, chopped
1 garlic clove, crushed
15ml/1 tbsp plain flour
15ml/1 tbsp paprika, plus extra
   to garnish
400g/14oz can chopped tomatoes
2 red peppers, halved and seeded
150ml/¼ pint/⅔ cup crème fraîche
salt and black pepper
buttered noodles, to serve

1 Preheat the oven to 140°C/275°F/ Gas 1. Heat the oil in a large flameproof casserole and brown the meat in batches. Remove the meat from the casserole using a slotted spoon.

2 Add the onions and garlic and fry gently until softened. Stir in the flour and paprika and continue cooking for a further 1–2 minutes, stirring.

3 Return the meat and any juices that have collected on the plate to the casserole, then add the chopped tomatoes and seasoning. Bring to the boil, stirring, then cover and cook in the oven for 2½ hours.

4 Meanwhile, place the peppers skin-side up on a grill rack and grill until the skins have blistered and charred. Cool, then peel off the skins. Cut the flesh into strips. Add to the casserole and cook for a further 15–30 minutes, or until the meat is tender.

5 Stir in the crème fraîche and sprinkle with a little paprika. Serve hot with buttered noodles.

--- COOK'S TIP ---

Take care when browning the meat and add only a few pieces at a time. If you overcrowd the pan, steam is created and the meat will never brown!

Beef and Aubergine Curry

INGREDIENTS

Serves 6

120ml/4fl oz/½ cup sunflower oil
2 onions, thinly sliced
2.5cm/1in fresh root ginger, sliced and
    cut in matchsticks
1 garlic clove, crushed
2 fresh red chillies, seeded and very
    finely sliced
2.5cm/1in fresh turmeric, peeled and
    crushed, or 5ml/1 tsp
    ground turmeric
1 lemon grass stem, lower part sliced
    finely, top bruised
675g/1½ lb braising steak, cut in even-
    size strips
400ml/14fl oz can coconut milk
300ml/½ pint/1¼ cups water
1 aubergine, sliced and patted dry
5ml/1 tsp tamarind pulp, soaked in
    60ml/4 tbsp warm water
salt and freshly ground black pepper
finely sliced chilli, (optional) and Deep-
    fried Onions, to garnish
boiled rice, to serve

1 Heat half the oil and fry the
onions, ginger and garlic until they
give off a rich aroma. Add the chillies,
turmeric and the lower part of the
lemon grass. Push to one side and then
turn up the heat and add the steak,
stirring until the meat changes colour.

COOK'S TIP

If you want to make this curry, *Gulai
Terung Dengan Daging,* ahead, prepare to
the end of step 2·and finish later.

---

2 Add the coconut milk, water,
lemon grass top and seasoning to
taste. Cover and simmer gently for
1½ hours, or until the meat is tender.

3 Towards the end of the cooking
time heat the remaining oil in a
frying pan. Fry the aubergine slices
until brown on both sides.

4 Add the browned aubergine slices
to the beef curry and cook for a
further 15 minutes. Stir gently from
time to time. Strain the tamarind and
stir the juice into the curry. Taste and
adjust the seasoning. Put into a warm
serving dish. Garnish with the sliced
chilli, if using, and Deep-fried Onions,
and serve with boiled rice.

Herby Lamb Hot-pot

Browning the lamb and kidneys, plus all the extra vegetables and herbs, adds flavour to the traditional basic ingredients.

INGREDIENTS

Serves 4

40g/1½oz/3 tbsp dripping, or 45ml/ 3 tbsp oil
8 middle neck lamb chops, about 1kg/2lb total weight
175g/6oz lamb's kidneys, cut into large pieces
1kg/2lb potatoes, thinly sliced
3 carrots, thickly sliced
450g/1lb leeks, sliced
3 celery sticks, sliced
15ml/1 tbsp chopped fresh thyme
30ml/2 tbsp chopped fresh parsley
small sprig of rosemary
600ml/1 pint/2½ cups veal stock
salt and black pepper

1 Preheat the oven to 170°C/325°F/ Gas 3. Heat the dripping or oil in a frying pan and brown the chops and kidneys in batches, then reserve the fat.

2 In a large casserole, make alternate layers of lamb chops, kidneys, three-quarters of the potatoes and the carrots, leeks and celery, sprinkling the herbs and seasoning over each layer as you go. Tuck the rosemary sprig down the side.

3 Arrange the remaining potatoes on top. Pour over the stock, brush with the reserved fat, then cover and bake for 2½ hours. Increase the oven temperature to 220°C/425°F/Gas 7. Uncover and cook for 30 minutes.

Pork Chops with Plums

INGREDIENTS

Serves 4

450g/1lb ripe plums, halved and stoned
300ml/½ pint/1¼ cups apple juice
40g/1½oz/3 tbsp butter
15ml/1 tbsp oil
4 pork chops, about 200g/7oz each
1 onion, finely chopped
grated nutmeg
salt and black pepper
fresh sage leave, to garnish

1 Heat the butter and oil in a large frying pan and fry the chops until brown on both sides, then transfer them to a plate.

2 Meanwhile, simmer the plums in the apple juice until tender. Strain off and reserve the juice, then purée half the plums with a little of the juice.

3 Add the onion to the pan and cook gently until soft, but not coloured. Return the chops to the pan. Pour over the plum purée and all the juice.

4 Simmer, uncovered, for 10–15 minutes, until the chops are cooked through. Add the remaining plums to the pan, then add the nutmeg and seasoning. Warm the sauce through over a medium heat and serve garnished with fresh sage leaves.

COOK'S TIP

Use boneless pork steaks in place of the chops, if you like.

Spiced Lamb with Apricots

INGREDIENTS

Serves 4

115g/4oz/½ cup ready-to-eat dried
  apricots
50g/2oz/⅓ cup seedless raisins
2.5ml/½ tsp saffron strands
150ml/¼ pint/⅔ cup orange juice
15ml/1 tbsp red wine vinegar
30–45ml/2–3 tbsp olive oil
1.5 kg/3lb leg of lamb, boned
  and cubed
1 onion, chopped
2 garlic cloves, crushed
10ml/2 tsp ground cumin
1.25ml/¼ tsp ground cloves
15ml/1 tbsp ground coriander
30ml/2 tbsp plain flour
600ml/1 pint/2½ cups lamb stock
45ml/3 tbsp chopped fresh coriander
salt and black pepper
saffron rice mixed with toasted
  almonds and chopped fresh
  coriander, to serve

1 Mix together the dried apricots, raisins, saffron, orange juice and vinegar in a bowl. Cover and leave to soak for 2–3 hours.

2 Preheat the oven to 160°C/325°F/ Gas 3. Heat 30ml/2 tbsp oil in a large flameproof casserole and brown the lamb in batches. Remove and set aside. Add the onion and garlic with a little more of the remaining oil, if necessary, and cook until softened.

3 Stir in the spices and flour and cook for a further 1–2 minutes. Return the meat to the casserole. Stir in the stock, fresh coriander and the soaked fruit with its liquid. Add seasoning, then bring to the boil.

4 Cover the casserole and cook for 1½ hours (adding a little extra stock if necessary), or until the lamb is tender. Serve with saffron rice mixed with toasted almonds and fresh coriander.

Sausage and Bean Ragoût

An economical and nutritious main course that children will love. Garlic and herb bread makes an ideal accompaniment.

INGREDIENTS

Serves 4

350g/12oz/2 cups dried flageolet
  beans, soaked overnight
45ml/3 tbsp olive oil
1 onion, finely chopped
2 garlic cloves, crushed
450g/1lb good-quality chunky
  sausages, skinned and thickly sliced
15ml/1 tbsp tomato purée
30ml/2 tbsp fresh chopped parsley
15ml/1 tbsp fresh chopped thyme
400g/14oz can chopped tomatoes
salt and black pepper
chopped fresh thyme and parsley,
to garnish

1 Drain and rinse the soaked beans and place them in a pan with enough water to cover. Bring to the boil, cover the pan and simmer for about 1 hour, or until tender. Drain the beans and set aside.

2 Heat the oil and fry the onion, garlic and sausages until golden.

3 Stir in the tomato purée, chopped parsley and thyme, tomatoes and seasoning, then bring to the boil.

4 Add the beans, then cover and cook gently for about 15 minutes, stirring occasionally, until the sausages are cooked through. Garnish with extra chopped fresh herbs and serve.

Beef in Guinness

INGREDIENTS

Serves 6

1kg/2lb chuck steak, cut into 4cm/
   1½in cubes
plain flour, for coating
45ml/3 tbsp oil
1 large onion, sliced
1 carrot, thinly sliced
2 celery sticks, thinly sliced
10ml/2 tsp sugar
5ml/1 tsp English mustard powder
15ml/1 tbsp tomato purée
2.5 x 7.5cm/1 x 3in strip orange rind
bouquet garni
600ml/1 pint/2½ cups Guinness
salt and black pepper

1 Toss the beef in flour to coat. Heat 30ml/2 tbsp oil in a large, shallow pan, then cook the beef in batches until lightly browned. Transfer to a bowl.

2 Add the remaining oil to the pan, then cook the onions until well browned, adding the carrot and celery towards the end.

3 Stir in the sugar, mustard, tomato purée, orange rind, Guinness and seasoning, then add the bouquet garni and bring to the boil. Return the meat, and any juices in the bowl, to the pan; add water, if necessary, so the meat is covered. Cover the pan tightly and cook gently for 2–2½ hours, until the meat is very tender.

Steak, Kidney and Mushroom Pie

INGREDIENTS

Serves 4

30ml/2 tbsp oil
1 onion, chopped
115g/4oz bacon, chopped
500g/1¼lb chuck steak, diced
30ml/2 tbsp plain flour
115g/4oz lamb's kidneys
400ml/14fl oz/1⅔ cups beef stock
large bouquet garni
115g/4oz button mushrooms
225g/8oz ready-made puff pastry
beaten egg, to glaze
salt and black pepper

1 Preheat the oven to 160°C/325°F/ Gas 3. Heat the oil in a heavy-based pan, then cook the bacon and onion until lightly browned.

2 Toss the steak in the flour. Stir the meat into the pan in batches and cook, stirring, until browned.

3 Toss the kidneys in flour and add to to the pan with the bouquet garni. Transfer to a casserole dish, then pour in the stock, cover and cook in the oven for 2 hours. Stir in the mushrooms and seasoning and leave to cool.

4 Preheat the oven to 220°C/425°F/ Gas 7. Roll out the pastry to about 2cm/¾in larger than the top of a 1.2 litre/2 pint/5 cup pie dish. Cut off a narrow strip from the pastry and fit around the dampened rim of the dish. Brush the pastry strip with water.

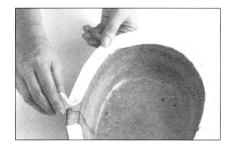

5 Tip the meat mixture, into the dish. Lay the pastry over the dish, press the edges together to seal, then knock them up with the back of a knife.

6 Make a small slit in the pastry, brush with beaten egg and bake for 20 minutes. Lower the oven temperature to 180°C/350°F/Gas 4 and bake for a further 20 minutes, until the pastry is risen, golden and crisp.

Pheasant with Apples

Pheasant is worth buying as it is low in fat, full of flavour, and never dry when cooked like this.

INGREDIENTS 🍎

Serves 4
1 pheasant
2 small onions, quartered
3 celery stalks, thickly sliced
2 red eating apples, thickly sliced
120ml/4fl oz/½ cup stock
15ml/1 tbsp clear honey
30ml/2 tbsp Worcestershire sauce
ground nutmeg
2 tbsp toasted hazelnuts
salt and black pepper

1 Preheat the oven to 180°C/350°F/ Gas 4. Sauté the pheasant without fat in a non-stick pan, turning occasionally until golden. Remove and keep hot.

2 Sauté the onions and celery in the pan to brown lightly. Spoon into a casserole and place the pheasant on top. Tuck the apple slices around it.

3 Spoon over the stock, honey, and Worcestershire sauce. Sprinkle with nutmeg, salt and pepper, cover, and bake for 1¼–1½ hours or until tender. Sprinkle with nuts and serve hot.

COOK'S TIP
Choose a firm variety of eating apple for this recipe, less acidic fruits hold their shape best.

Cider-baked Rabbit

Rabbit is a low fat meat and an economical choice for family meals. Chicken pieces may be used as an alternative.

INGREDIENTS 🍎

Serves 4
450g/1lb rabbit pieces
15ml/1 tbsp plain flour
5ml/1 tsp dry mustard
3 medium leeks, thickly sliced
250ml/8fl oz/1 cup dry cider
2 sprigs rosemary
salt and black pepper
fresh rosemary, to garnish

1 Preheat the oven to 180°C/350°F/ Gas 4. Place the rabbit pieces in a bowl and sprinkle over the flour and mustard. Toss to coat evenly.

2 Arrange the rabbit in one layer in a wide casserole. Blanch the leeks in boiling water, then drain and add to the casserole.

3 Add the cider, rosemary, and sea-soning, cover, then bake for 1–1¼ hours, or until the rabbit is tender. Garnish with fresh rosemary, and serve with baked potatoes and vegetables.

VARIATION
To make Cider-baked Chicken, substitute small chicken joints, such as thighs or drumsticks for the rabbit pieces.

Barbecued Jerk Chicken

Jerk refers to the blend of herb and spice seasoning rubbed into meat, before it is roasted over charcoal sprinkled with pimiento berries. In Jamaica, jerk seasoning was originally used only for pork, but jerked chicken is equally good.

INGREDIENTS

Serves 4
8 chicken pieces

For the marinade
5ml/1 tsp ground allspice
5ml/1 tsp ground cinnamon
5ml/1 tsp dried thyme
1.5ml/¼ tsp freshly grated nutmeg
10ml/2 tsp demerara sugar
2 garlic cloves, crushed
15ml/1 tbsp finely chopped onion
15ml/1 tbsp chopped spring onion
15ml/1 tbsp vinegar
30ml/2 tbsp oil
15ml/1 tbsp lime juice
1 hot chilli pepper, chopped
salt and freshly ground black pepper
salad leaves, to serve

1 Combine all the marinade ingredients in a small bowl. Using a fork, mash them together well to form a thick paste.

2 Lay the chicken pieces on a plate or board and make several lengthways slits in the flesh. Rub the seasoning all over the chicken and into the slits.

3 Place the chicken pieces in a dish, cover with clear film and marinate overnight in the fridge.

4 Shake off any excess seasoning from the chicken. Brush with oil and either place on a baking sheet or on a barbecue grill if barbecuing. Cook under a preheated grill for 45 minutes, turning often. Or, if barbecuing, light the coals and when ready, cook over the coals for 30 minutes, turning often. Serve hot with salad leaves.

COOK'S TIP

The flavour is best if you marinate the chicken overnight. Sprinkle the charcoal with aromatic herbs such as bay leaves for even more flavour.

Stir-fried Turkey with Mange-tout

INGREDIENTS

Serves 4

30ml/2 tbsp sesame oil
90ml/6 tbsp lemon juice
1 garlic clove, crushed
1cm/½in piece fresh root ginger,
  peeled and grated
5ml/1 tsp clear honey
450g/1lb turkey fillets, cut into strips
115g/4oz mange-tout, trimmed
30ml/2 tbsp groundnut oil
50g/2oz/⅓ cup cashew nuts
6 spring onions, cut into strips
225g/8oz can water chestnuts, drained
  and thinly sliced
salt
saffron rice, to serve

1 Mix together the sesame oil, lemon juice, garlic, ginger and honey in a shallow non-metallic dish. Add the turkey and mix well. Cover and leave to marinate for 3–4 hours.

2 Blanch the mange-tout in boiling salted water for 1 minute. Drain and refresh under cold running water.

3 Drain the marinade from the turkey strips and reserve the marinade. Heat the groundnut oil in a wok or large frying pan, add the cashew nuts and stir-fry for about 1–2 minutes until golden brown. Remove the cashew nuts from the wok or frying pan using a slotted spoon and set aside.

4 Add the turkey and stir-fry for 3–4 minutes, until golden brown. Add the spring onions, mange-tout, water chestnuts and the reserved marinade. Cook for a few minutes, until the turkey is tender and the sauce is bubbling and hot. Stir in the cashew nuts and serve with saffron rice.

Tandoori Chicken Kebabs

This dish originates from the plains of the Punjab at the foot of the Himalayas. There food is traditionally cooked in clay ovens known as tandoors – hence the name.

INGREDIENTS

Serves 4

4 boneless, skinless chicken breasts
   (about 175g/6oz each)
15ml/1 tbsp lemon juice
45ml/3 tbsp tandoori paste
45ml/3 tbsp natural yogurt
1 garlic clove, crushed
30ml/2 tbsp chopped fresh coriander
1 small onion, cut into wedges and
   separated into layers
a little oil, for brushing
salt and black pepper
fresh coriander sprigs, to garnish
pilau rice and naan bread, to serve

1 Chop the chicken breasts into 2.5cm/1in cubes, place in a bowl and add the lemon juice, tandoori paste, yogurt, garlic, coriander and seasoning. Cover and leave to marinate in the fridge for 2–3 hours.

2 Preheat the grill. Thread alternate pieces of marinated chicken and onion on to four skewers.

3 Brush the onions with a little oil, lay on a grill rack and cook under a high heat for 10–12 minutes, turning once. Garnish the kebabs with fresh coriander and serve at once with pilau rice and naan bread.

> ——— COOK'S TIP ———
>
> Use chopped, boned and skinless chicken thighs, or turkey breasts for a cheaper alternative.

Chinese Chicken with Cashew Nuts

INGREDIENTS

Serves 4

4 boneless chicken breasts (about
   175g/6oz each), skinned and sliced
   into strips
3 garlic cloves, crushed
60ml/4 tbsp soy sauce
30ml/2 tbsp cornflour
225g/8oz dried egg noodles
45ml/3 tbsp groundnut or sunflower oil
15ml/1 tbsp sesame oil
115g/4oz/1 cup roasted cashew nuts
6 spring onions, cut into 5cm/2in
   pieces and halved lengthways
spring onion curls and a little chopped
   red chilli, to garnish

1 Place the chicken in a bowl with the garlic, soy sauce and cornflour and mix until the chicken is well coated. Cover and chill for about 30 minutes.

2 Meanwhile, bring a pan of water to the boil and add the egg noodles. Turn off the heat and leave to stand for 5 minutes. Drain well and reserve.

3 Heat the oils in a large frying pan or wok and add the chilled chicken and marinade juices. Stir-fry on a high heat for about 3–4 minutes, or until golden brown.

4 Add the cashew nuts and spring onions to the pan or wok and stir-fry for 2–3 minutes.

5 Add the drained noodles and stir-fry for a further 2 minutes. Toss the noodles well and serve immediately, garnished with the spring onion curls and chopped chilli.

Chicken Parcels with Herb Butter

INGREDIENTS

Serves 4

4 chicken breast fillets, skinned
150g/5oz/10 tbsp butter, softened
90ml/6 tbsp chopped fresh mixed
   herbs, such as thyme, parsley,
   oregano and rosemary
5ml/1 tsp lemon juice
5 large sheets filo pastry, defrosted
   if frozen
1 egg, beaten
30ml/2 tbsp grated Parmesan cheese
salt and black pepper

1 Season the chicken fillets and fry in 25g/1oz/2 tbsp of the butter to seal and brown lightly. Allow to cool.

2 Preheat the oven to 190°C/375°F/ Gas 5. Put the remaining butter, the herbs, lemon juice and seasoning in a food processor and process until smooth. Melt half the herb butter.

3 Take one sheet of filo pastry and brush with herb butter. Fold the filo pastry sheet in half and brush again with butter. Place a chicken fillet about 2.5cm/1in from the top end.

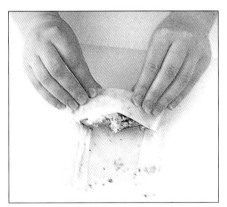

4 Dot the chicken with a quarter of the remaining herb butter. Fold in the sides of the pastry, then roll up to enclose it completely. Place seam-side down on a lightly greased baking sheet. Repeat with the other chicken fillets.

5 Brush the filo parcels with beaten egg. Cut the last sheet of filo into strips, then scrunch and arrange on top. Brush the parcels once again with the egg glaze, then sprinkle with Parmesan. Bake for about 35–40 minutes, until golden brown. Serve hot.

Roast Chicken with Celeriac

INGREDIENTS

Serves 4

1.6kg/3½lb chicken
15g/½oz/1 tbsp butter

For the stuffing

450g/1lb celeriac, chopped
25g/1oz/2 tbsp butter
3 slices bacon, chopped
1 onion, finely chopped
leaves from 1 thyme sprig, chopped
leaves from 1 small tarragon sprig,
   chopped
30ml/2 tbsp chopped fresh parsley
75g/3oz/1½ cups fresh brown
   breadcrumbs
dash of Worcestershire sauce
1 egg
salt and black pepper

1 To make the stuffing, cook the celeriac in boiling water until tender. Drain well and chop finely.

2 Heat the butter in a saucepan, then gently cook the bacon and onion until the onion is soft. Stir the celeriac and herb leaves into the pan and cook, stirring occasionally, for 2–3 minutes. Meanwhile, preheat the oven to 200°C/400°F/Gas 6.

——— COOK'S TIP ———

Roll any excess stuffing into small balls and bake in a buttered ovenproof dish with the chicken for 20–30 minutes until golden brown.

3 Remove the pan from the heat and stir in the fresh breadcrumbs, Worcestershire sauce, seasoning and sufficient egg to bind. Use to stuff the neck end of the chicken. Season the bird's skin, then rub with the butter.

4 Roast the chicken, basting occasionally with the juices, for 1¼–1½ hours, until the juices run clear when the thickest part of the leg is pierced.

5 Turn off the oven, prop the door open slightly and allow the chicken to rest for 10 minutes before carving.

Chicken, Leek and Parsley Pie

INGREDIENTS

Serves 4–6

For the pastry
275g/10oz/2½ cups plain flour
pinch of salt
200g/7oz/7/8 cup butter, diced
2 egg yolks

For the filling
3 part-boned chicken breasts
flavouring ingredients (bouquet garni,
    black peppercorns, onion and carrot)
50g/2oz/4 tbsp butter
2 leeks, thinly sliced
50g/2oz Cheddar cheese, grated
25g/1oz Parmesan cheese, finely grated
45ml/3 tbsp chopped fresh parsley
30ml/2 tbsp wholegrain mustard
5ml/1 tsp cornflour
300ml/½ pint/1¼ cups double cream
salt and black pepper
beaten egg, to glaze
mixed green salad, to serve

1 To make the pastry, first sift the flour and salt. Blend together the butter and egg yolks in a food processor until creamy. Add the flour and process until the mixture is just coming together. Add about 15ml/1 tbsp cold water and process for a few seconds more. Turn out on to a lightly floured surface and knead lightly. Wrap in clear film and chill for about 1 hour.

2 Meanwhile, poach the chicken breasts in water to cover, with the flavouring ingredients added, until tender. Leave to cool in the liquid.

3 Preheat the oven to 200°C/400°F/ Gas 6. Divide the pastry into two pieces, one slightly larger than the other. Roll out the larger piece on a lightly floured surface and use to line a 18 x 28cm/7 x 11in baking dish or tin. Prick the base with a fork and bake for 15 minutes. Leave to cool.

4 Lift the cooled chicken from the poaching liquid and discard the skins and bones. Cut the chicken flesh into strips, then set aside.

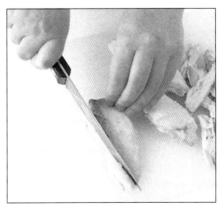

5 Melt the butter in a frying pan and fry the leeks over a low heat, stirring occasionally, until soft.

6 Stir in the Cheddar, Parmesan and chopped parsley. Spread half the leek mixture over the cooked pastry base, leaving a border all the way round. Cover the leek mixture with the chicken strips, then top with the remaining leek mixture.

7 Mix together the mustard, cornflour and cream in a small bowl. Add seasoning to taste. Pour over the filling.

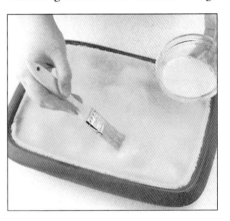

8 Moisten the edges of the cooked pastry base. Roll out the remaining pastry and use to cover the pie. Brush with beaten egg and bake for 30–40 minutes until golden and crisp. Serve hot, cut into square portions, with a mixed green salad.

COOK'S TIP

This pastry is quite fragile and may break; the high fat content, however, means you can patch it together by pressing pieces of pastry trimmings into any cracks.

FISH AND VEGETARIAN DISHES

This collection of recipes presents some old favourites as well as new ideas culled from international cuisine. Try the simple but rewarding Spaghetti with Tuna Sauce or splash out with Salmon with Watercress Sauce for a dinner party. For vegetarians and the health-conscious alike, Root Vegetable Couscous, Potato and Red Pepper Frittata and Red Bean Chilli make delicious week-day meals.

Baked Cod with Tomatoes

For the very best flavour, use firm ripe tomatoes for the sauce and make sure it is thick before spooning over the cod.

INGREDIENTS

Serves 4
30ml/2 tbsp olive oil
1 onion, chopped
2 garlic cloves, finely chopped
450g/1lb tomatoes, peeled, seeded and chopped
5ml/1 tsp tomato purée
60ml/4 tbsp dry white wine
60ml/4 tbsp chopped flat leaf parsley
4 cod cutlets
30ml/2 tbsp dried breadcrumbs
salt and black pepper
new potatoes and green salad, to serve

1 Preheat the oven to 190°C/375°F/ Gas 5. Heat the oil in a pan and fry the onion for about 5 minutes. Add the garlic, tomatoes, tomato purée, wine and seasoning. Bring just to the boil, then reduce the heat slightly and cook, uncovered, for 15–20 minutes until thick. Stir in the parsley.

2 Place the cod cutlets in a shallow greased ovenproof dish and spoon an equal quantity of the tomato sauce on to each piece. Sprinkle the dried breadcrumbs over the top.

3 Bake for 20–30 minutes, basting occasionally, until the breadcrumbs are golden and crisp. Serve with new potatoes and a green salad.

Sole with Cider and Cream

INGREDIENTS

Serves 4
50g/2oz/4 tbsp butter
1 onion, chopped
8 lemon sole fillets, about 115g/4oz each, skinned
300ml/½ pint/1¼ cups dry cider
150ml/¼ pint/⅔ cup fish stock
few parsley stalks
115g/4oz button mushrooms, sliced
115g/4oz cooked, peeled prawns, defrosted if frozen
15ml/1 tbsp each plain flour and butter, blended together to make a beurre manié
120ml/4fl oz/½ cup double cream
salt and black pepper
chopped fresh parsley, to garnish

1 Melt 25g/1oz/2 tbsp of the butter in a frying pan with a lid. Add the chopped onion and fry gently, stirring occasionally, until softened.

2 Lightly season the fish, then fold each into three. Place the fish in the pan, and pour over the cider and stock. Tuck in the parsley stalks. Bring to simmering point, cover and cook for 7–10 minutes, until the fish is tender.

3 Meanwhile, melt the remaining butter and cook the mushrooms in a separate pan until tender. Transfer the fish to a warmed serving plate and scatter over the prawns. Cover and keep warm while making the sauce.

4 Strain the fish cooking juices and return to the pan. Boil rapidly until slightly reduced. Add the beurre manié a little at a time, stirring until the sauce has thickened. Stir in the cream and seasoning to taste, then heat gently.

5 Spoon the cooked mushrooms over the fish, then pour over the cream sauce. Sprinkle with chopped fresh parsley and serve at once.

Mediterranean Fish Stew

INGREDIENTS

Serves 4

225g/8oz/2 cups cooked prawns in shells
450g/1lb mixed white fish fillets such as cod, whiting, haddock, mullet or monkfish skinned and chopped (reserve skins for the stock)
45ml/3 tbsp olive oil
1 onion, chopped
1 leek, sliced
1 carrot, diced
1 garlic clove, chopped
2.5ml/½ tsp ground turmeric
150ml/¼ pint/⅔ cup dry white wine or cider
400g/14oz can chopped tomatoes
sprig of fresh parsley, thyme and fennel
1 bay leaf
a small piece of orange peel
1 prepared squid, body cut into rings and tentacles chopped
12 mussels in shells
salt and black pepper
30–45ml/2–3 tbsp Parmesan cheese shavings, to sprinkle
chopped fresh parsley, to garnish

For the rouille sauce

2 slices white bread, crusts removed
2 garlic cloves, crushed
½ fresh red chilli
15ml/1 tbsp tomato purée
45–60ml/3–4 tbsp olive oil

1 Peel the prawns leaving the tails on; cover and chill. Place all the prawn trimmings and fish trimmings in a pan and cover with 450ml/¾ pint/1⅞ cups water. Bring to the boil, then cover and simmer for about 30 minutes. Strain and reserve the stock.

2 Heat the oil in a large saucepan and add the onion, leek, carrot and garlic. Fry gently for 6–7 minutes, then stir in the turmeric. Pour on the white wine, tomatoes and juice, the reserved fish stock, the herbs and orange peel. Bring to the boil, then cover and simmer gently for about 20 minutes.

3 Meanwhile, prepare the rouille sauce. Blend the bread in a food processor with the garlic, chilli and tomato purée. With the motor running, pour in the oil in a thin drizzle until the mixture is smooth and thickened.

4 Add the fish and seafood to the pan and simmer for 5–6 minutes, or until the fish is opaque and the mussels open. Remove the bay leaf and peel. Season the stew and serve in bowls with a spoonful of the rouille sauce, and sprinkled with Parmesan and parsley.

Salmon with Watercress Sauce

Fresh watercress gives the sauce a wonderful colour.

INGREDIENTS

Serves 4

300ml/½ pint/1¼ cups crème fraîche
30ml/2 tbsp chopped fresh tarragon
25g/1oz/2 tbsp unsalted butter
15ml/1 tbsp sunflower oil
4 salmon fillets, skinned and boned
1 garlic clove, crushed
100ml/3½fl oz/½ cup dry white wine
1 bunch watercress
salt and black pepper

1 Gently heat the crème fraîche in a small pan until just beginning to boil. Remove the pan from the heat and stir in half the tarragon. Leave the herb cream to infuse while cooking the fish.

2 Heat the butter and oil in a frying pan, add the salmon and fry for 3–5 minutes on each side. Remove from the pan and keep warm.

3 Add the garlic and fry for 1 minute, then pour in the wine and let it bubble until reduced to about 15ml/1 tbsp.

4 Meanwhile, strip the leaves off the watercress stalks and chop finely. Discard any damaged leaves. (Save the watercress stalks for soup, if you like.)

5 Strain the herb cream into the pan and cook for a few minutes, stirring until the sauce has thickened. Stir in the remaining tarragon and watercress, then cook for a few minutes, until wilted but still bright green. Season and serve at once, spooned over the salmon.

Tagliatelle with Hazelnut Pesto

Hazelnuts are lower in fat than other nuts, which makes them useful for this reduced-fat alternative to pesto sauce.

INGREDIENTS 🍎

Serves 4

2 garlic cloves, crushed
25g/1oz/1 cup fresh basil leaves
25g/1oz/¼ cup hazelnuts
200g/7oz/⅞ cup skimmed milk soft cheese
225g/8oz dried tagliatelle, or 450g/1lb fresh
salt and black pepper

1 Place the garlic, basil, hazelnuts, and cheese in a food processor or blender and process to a thick paste.

2 Cook the tagliatelle in lightly salted boiling water until just tender, then drain well.

3 Spoon the sauce into the hot pasta, tossing until melted. Sprinkle with pepper and serve hot.

—— COOK'S TIP ——

Italian ricotta cheese makes a good, though less low-fat, alternative to skimmed milk soft cheese in this recipe.

Spaghetti with Tuna Sauce

A speedy, and very tasty, mid-week meal, which can also be made with other pasta shapes.

INGREDIENTS 🍎

Serves 4

225g/8oz dried spaghetti, or 450g/1lb fresh
1 garlic clove, crushed
400g/14oz can chopped tomatoes
425g/15oz can tuna in water, drained and flaked
2.5ml/½ tsp chilli sauce (optional)
4 pitted black olives, chopped
salt and black pepper

—— COOK'S TIP ——

If fresh tuna is available, use 450g/1lb, cut into small chunks, and add after step 2. Simmer for 6–8 minutes, then add the chilli sauce, olives, and pasta.

1 Cook the spaghetti in lightly salted boiling water for 12 minutes or until just tender. Drain well and keep hot.

2 Add the garlic and tomatoes to the saucepan and bring to a boil. Simmer, uncovered, for 2–3 minutes.

3 Add the tuna, chilli sauce, if using, olives, and spaghetti. Heat well, add the seasoning, and serve hot.

—— VARIATION ——

To make a less hot, herby version of this dish, omit the chilli sauce and add 60ml/ 4 tbsp chopped mixed fresh herbs instead.

Tomato Risotto

Use plum tomatoes in this dish for their fresh vibrant flavour and firm texture.

INGREDIENTS

Serves 4

675g/1½lb firm ripe tomatoes, preferably plum
50g/2oz/4 tbsp butter
1 onion, finely chopped
about 1.2 litres/2 pints/5 cups vegetable stock
275g/10oz/1½ cups arborio rice
400g/14oz can cannellini beans, drained
50g/2oz Parmesan cheese, finely grated
salt and black pepper
10–12 basil leaves, shredded, and shavings of Parmesan cheese, to serve

1 Halve the tomatoes and scoop out the seeds into a sieve placed over a bowl. Press the seeds with a spoon to extract all the juice. Set aside.

2 Grill the tomatoes skin-side up until the skins are blackened and blistered. Rub off the skins and dice the flesh.

3 Melt the butter in a large pan, add the onion and cook for 5 minutes until beginning to soften. Add the tomatoes, the reserved juice and seasoning, then cook, stirring occasionally, for about 10 minutes.

4 Meanwhile, bring the vegetable stock to the boil in another pan.

5 Add the rice to the tomatoes and stir to coat. Add a ladleful of the stock and stir gently until absorbed. Repeat, adding a ladleful of stock at a time, until all the stock is absorbed and the rice is tender and creamy.

6 Stir in the cannellini beans and grated Parmesan and heat through for a few minutes.

7 Just before serving the risotto, sprinkle each portion with shredded basil leaves and shavings of Parmesan.

Potato Cakes with Goat's Cheese

INGREDIENTS

Serves 2–4

450g/1lb potatoes
10ml/2 tsp chopped fresh thyme
1 garlic clove, crushed
2 spring onions (including the green
 parts), finely chopped
30ml/2 tbsp olive oil
50g/2oz/4 tbsp unsalted butter
2 x 65g/2½oz Crottins de Chavignol
 (firm goat's cheeses)
salt and black pepper
salad leaves, such as curly endive,
 radicchio and lamb's lettuce, tossed
 in walnut dressing, to serve
thyme sprigs, to garnish

1 Peel and coarsely grate the potatoes. Using your hands squeeze out all the excess moisture, then carefully combine with the chopped thyme, garlic, spring onions and seasoning.

2 Heat half the oil and butter in a non-stick frying pan. Add two large spoonfuls of the potato mixture, spacing them well apart, and press firmly down with a spatula. Cook for 3–4 minutes on each side until golden.

3 Drain the potato cakes on kitchen paper and keep warm in a low oven. Make two more potato cakes in the same way with the remaining mixture. Meanwhile, preheat the grill.

4 Cut the cheese in half horizontally and place one half, cut side up, on each potato cake. Grill for 2–3 minutes until golden. Transfer the potato cakes to serving plates and arrange the salad leaves around them. Garnish with thyme sprigs and serve at once.

Twice-baked Cheddar Soufflés

This is an ace of a recipe for busy people and really easy to make. The soufflés can be prepared well in advance, then simply reheated just before serving.

INGREDIENTS

Serves 4

300ml/½ pint/1¼ cups milk
flavouring ingredients (a few onion slices, 1 bay leaf and 4 black peppercorns)
65g/2½oz/5 tbsp butter
40g/1½oz/⅓ cup plain flour
115g/4oz mature Cheddar cheese, grated
1.25ml/¼ tsp mustard powder
3 eggs, separated
20ml/4 tsp chopped fresh parsley
250ml/8fl oz/1 cup double cream
salt and black pepper

1 Preheat the oven to 180°C/350°F/ Gas 4. Put the milk in a pan with the flavouring ingredients. Bring slowly to the boil, then strain into a jug.

COOK'S TIP

Don't attempt to unmould the soufflés until they have cooled, when they will be firmer and easier to handle. They can be kept chilled for up to 8 hours. Use snipped fresh chives instead of the parsley, if you like.

2 Melt the butter in the rinsed-out pan and use a little to grease four 150ml/¼ pint/⅔ cup ramekins.

3 Stir the flour into the remaining butter in the pan and cook for 1 minute. Gradually add the hot milk, then bring to the boil, stirring until thickened and smooth. Cook, stirring all the time, for 2 minutes.

4 Remove the pan from the heat and stir in 75g/3oz of the grated cheese and the mustard powder. Beat in the egg yolks, followed by the chopped parsley, and season to taste with salt and black pepper.

5 Whisk the egg whites in a large bowl until stiff but not dry. Mix in a spoonful of the egg whites to lighten the cheese mixture, then gently fold in the remaining egg whites.

6 Spoon the soufflé mixture into the ramekins, place in a roasting tin and pour in boiling water to come halfway up the sides. Bake the soufflés for 15–20 minutes until risen and set. Remove the ramekins immediately from the tin and allow the soufflés to sink and cool, until ready to serve.

7 When ready to serve, preheat the oven to 220°C/ 425°F/Gas 7. Carefully turn out the soufflés into a buttered shallow ovenproof dish or individual dishes. Season the cream and pour over the soufflés, then sprinkle over the remaining cheese.

8 Bake the soufflés for about 10–15 minutes, until risen and golden brown. Serve at once.

Root Vegetable Couscous

Cheap and plentiful, autumn's crop of flavourful root vegetables is perfect for this delicious vegetarian main course. The spiced red sauce is fairly fiery and is not for the faint hearted! If you prefer your food less hot, leave out the harissa.

INGREDIENTS

Serves 4

350g/12oz/2 cups couscous
45ml/3 tbsp olive oil
4 baby onions, halved
675g/1½lb mixed root vegetables, such as parsnips, carrots, swede, turnip, celeriac and sweet potatoes, cut into chunks
2 garlic cloves, crushed
pinch of saffron strands
2.5ml/½ tsp ground cinnamon
2.5ml/½ tsp ground ginger
2.5ml/½ tsp ground turmeric
5ml/1 tsp ground cumin
5ml/1 tsp ground coriander
15ml/1 tbsp tomato purée
450ml/¾ pint/1⅞ cups hot vegetable stock
1 small fennel bulb, quartered
115g/4oz/1 cup cooked or canned chick-peas
50g/2oz/⅓ cup seedless raisins
30ml/2 tbsp chopped fresh coriander
30ml/2 tbsp chopped fresh flat leaf parsley
salt and black pepper

For the spiced red sauce
15ml/1 tbsp olive oil
15ml/1 tbsp lemon juice
15ml/1 tbsp chopped fresh coriander
2.5–5ml/½–1 tsp harissa

1 Put the couscous in a bowl, cover with hot water and drain. Spread out on to a tray and leave for about 20 minutes, sprinkling over a little water every 5 minutes to keep the couscous grains moist.

2 Meanwhile, heat the oil in a large frying pan and fry the onions for about 3 minutes. Add the mixed root vegetables and fry gently for about 5 minutes, until softened.

3 Add the garlic and spices to the frying pan and cook for 1 minute, stirring. Transfer the vegetable mixture to a large deep saucepan.

4 Stir the tomato purée and stock into the vegetable mixture, then add the fennel, chick-peas, raisins, chopped fresh coriander and flat leaf parsley. Bring to the boil.

5 Fork the couscous to break up any lumps and put into a steamer lined with muslin and place the steamer over the vegetable mixture.

6 Cover the steamer with a lid or foil and simmer for 15–20 minutes, until the vegetables are tender and the couscous is piping hot.

7 To make the spiced red sauce, strain about 250ml/8fl oz/1 cup of the liquid from the vegetables into a small pan. Stir in the olive oil, lemon juice, coriander and harissa, to taste.

8 Spoon the couscous on to a serving plate and pile the vegetables on top. Serve at once, handing round the spiced red sauce separately.

COOK'S TIP

Harissa is a very fiery Tunisian chilli sauce. It can be bought ready-made in small cans from Middle-Eastern shops.

Potato and Red Pepper Frittata

Fresh herbs make all the difference in this simple but delicious recipe – parsley or chives could be substituted for the chopped mint.

INGREDIENTS

Serves 3–4

450g/1lb small new potatoes
6 eggs
30ml/2 tbsp chopped fresh mint
30ml/2 tbsp olive oil
1 onion, chopped
2 garlic cloves, crushed
2 red peppers, seeded and roughly chopped
salt and black pepper
mint sprigs, to garnish

1 Scrub the potatoes, then cook in a pan of boiling salted water until just tender. Drain the potatoes, leave to cool slightly, then cut into thick slices.

2 Whisk together the eggs, mint and seasoning in a bowl, then set aside. Heat the oil in a large frying pan.

3 Add the onion, garlic, peppers and potatoes to the pan and cook, stirring, for 5 minutes.

4 Pour the egg mixture over the vegetables and stir gently.

5 Push the mixture into the centre of the pan as it cooks to allow the liquid egg to run on to the base.

6 Once the egg mixture is lightly set, place the pan under a hot grill for 2–3 minutes, until golden brown. Serve hot or cold, cut into wedges and garnished with sprigs of mint.

Red Bean Chilli

This vegetarian chilli can be adapted to accommodate meat eaters by adding either minced beef or lamb in place of the lentils. Add the meat once the onions are soft and fry until nicely browned before adding the tomatoes.

INGREDIENTS

Serves 4

30ml/2 tbsp vegetable oil
1 onion, chopped
400g/14oz can chopped tomatoes
2 garlic cloves, crushed
300ml/½ pint/1¼ cups white wine
about 300ml/½ pint/1¼ cups
  vegetable stock
115g/4oz red lentils
2 thyme sprigs or 5ml/1 tsp dried
  thyme
10ml/2 tsp ground cumin
45ml/3 tbsp dark soy sauce
½ hot chilli pepper, finely chopped
5ml/1 tsp mixed spice
15ml/1 tbsp oyster sauce (optional)
225g/8oz can red kidney beans,
  drained
10ml/2 tsp sugar
salt

1 Heat the oil in a large saucepan and fry the onion over a moderate heat for a few minutes until slightly softened.

2 Add the tomatoes and garlic, cook for 10 minutes, then stir in the wine and stock.

3 Add the lentils, thyme, cumin, soy sauce, hot pepper, mixed spice and oyster sauce, if using.

4 Cover and simmer for 40 minutes or until the lentils are cooked, stirring occasionally and adding more water if the lentils begin to dry out.

5 Stir in the kidney beans and sugar and continue cooking for 10 minutes, adding a little extra stock or water if necessary. Season to taste with salt and serve hot with boiled rice and sweetcorn.

COOK'S TIP

Fiery chillies can irritate the skin, so always wash your hands well after handling them and take care not to touch your eyes. If you like really hot, spicy food, then add the seeds from the chilli, too.

SIDE DISHES AND SALADS

Anyone can cook up a few vegetables or rustle up a salad to accompany most meals, but occasionally some inspiration in the form of new ideas is called for. For a really elegant vegetable dish, try Parcels of Baked Baby Vegetables, or spice up a plate of left-over roast or cold meats from the deli with Spanish Chilli Potatoes. The recipe for Broccoli and Cauliflower Gratin is made using a delicious low-calorie sauce. Finally, there are four tempting salads that can be served either as accompaniments or alone as a healthy, light lunch.

Parcels of Baked Baby Vegetables

If baby vegetables are unavailable use larger vegetables cut into bite-sized pieces.

INGREDIENTS

Serves 2

50g/2oz/4 tbsp unsalted butter
30ml/2 tbsp chopped fresh mixed herbs
1 garlic clove
2.5ml/½ tsp grated lemon rind
30ml/2 tbsp olive oil
350–450g/12oz–1lb mixed baby vegetables, such as carrots, turnips, parsnips, fennel and patty-pan squash
6 baby onions, peeled
lemon juice (optional)
salt and black pepper
shavings of Pecorino or Parmesan cheese or soft goat's cheese, and crusty bread, to serve

1 Preheat the oven to 220°C/425°F/Gas 7. Put the butter, herbs, garlic and lemon rind in a food processor and process until blended. Season to taste.

2 Heat the oil in a frying pan or wok and stir-fry the vegetables for about 3 minutes, until lightly browned.

3 Divide the vegetables equally between two sheets of foil and dot with the herb butter. Close the parcels tightly and place on a baking sheet. Bake for 30–40 minutes, until just tender.

4 Carefully unwrap the parcels and add a squeeze of lemon juice, if needed, to perk up the flavours.

5 Serve the vegetables in the parcels or transfer to warmed soup plates. Spoon over the juices and accompany with the cheese and crusty bread.

Summer Vegetable Braise

Tender, young vegetables are ideal for quick cooking in a minimum of liquid. Use any mixture of the family's favourite vegetables, as long as they are of similar size.

INGREDIENTS 🍎

Serves 4

175g/6oz/2½ cups baby carrots
175g/6oz/2 cups sugar-snap peas or
    mange-tout
115g/4oz/1¼ cups baby corn
90ml/6 tbsp vegetable stock
10ml/2 tsp lime juice
salt and black pepper
chopped fresh parsley and snipped fresh
    chives, to garnish

1 Place the carrots, peas, and baby corn in a large heavy-based saucepan with the vegetable stock and lime juice. Bring to the boil.

2 Cover the pan and reduce the heat, then simmer for 6–8 minutes, shaking the pan occasionally, until the vegetables are just tender.

3 Season the vegetables to taste with salt and pepper, then stir in the chopped fresh parsley and snipped chives. Cook the vegetables for a few seconds more, stirring them once or twice until the herbs are well mixed, then serve at once.

--- COOK'S TIP ---

You can make this dish in the winter too, but cut larger, tougher vegetables into chunks and cook for slightly longer.

--- VARIATION ---

To make a more substantial dish, tip the cooked vegetables into a gratin dish and scatter with a mixture of grated cheese and breadcrumbs and grill until golden and bubbling.

Broccoli and Cauliflower Gratin

Broccoli and cauliflower make an attractive combination, and this dish is much lighter than the classic cheese sauce.

INGREDIENTS 🍎

Serves 4

1 small cauliflower (about 250g/9oz)
1 small head broccoli (about 250g/9oz)
150g/5oz/½ cup plain low fat yogurt
75g/3oz/1 cup grated low fat Cheddar cheese
5ml/1 tsp wholegrain mustard
30ml/2 tbsp wholemeal breadcrumbs
salt and black pepper

1 Break the cauliflower and broccoli into florets and cook in lightly salted, boiling water for 8–10 minutes, until just tender. Drain well and transfer to a flameproof dish.

2 Mix together the yogurt, grated cheese, and mustard, then season the mixture with pepper and spoon over the cauliflower and broccoli.

3 Sprinkle the breadcrumbs over the top and place under a grill until golden brown. Serve hot.

COOK'S TIP

When preparing the cauliflower and broccoli, discard the tougher part of the stalk, then break the florets into even-sized pieces, so they cook evenly.

Rice Pilaff

This simple pilaff will complement most main course dishes. Alter the dried and fresh herbs to suit your meal.

INGREDIENTS

Serves 6–8

40g/1½oz/3 tbsp butter or
   45–60ml/3–4 tbsp oil
1 onion, finely chopped
450g/1lb/generous 2¼ cups long
   grain rice
750ml/1¼ pints/3 cups vegetable stock
   or water
2.5ml/½ tsp dried thyme
1 small bay leaf
salt and ground black pepper
15–30ml/1–2 tbsp chopped fresh
   parsley, dill or snipped chives,
   to garnish

1 In a large heavy saucepan, melt the butter or heat the oil over a medium heat. Add the onion and cook for 2–3 minutes until just softened, stirring all the time.

2 Add the rice and cook for 1–2 minutes until the rice becomes translucent, stirring frequently. Do not allow to brown.

3 Add the stock or water, dried thyme and bay leaf and season with salt and pepper. Bring to the boil over a high heat, stirring frequently. Just as the rice begins to boil, cover the surface with a round of foil and put the lid on the saucepan. Reduce the heat to very low and cook for 20 minutes (do not lift the cover or stir). Serve hot, garnished with fresh herbs.

--- COOK'S TIP ---

Once cooked the rice will remain hot for about half an hour, if tightly covered. To reheat the rice, spoon it into a microwave-safe bowl, cover with pierced clear film and microwave on full power for about 5 minutes until hot.

Bombay Spiced Potatoes

This Indian potato dish uses a mixture of whole and ground spices. Look out for mustard and black onion seeds in specialist food shops.

INGREDIENTS

Serves 4

4 large potatoes (Maris Piper or King Edward), cubed
60ml/4 tbsp sunflower oil
1 garlic clove, finely chopped
10ml/2 tsp brown mustard seeds
5ml/1 tsp black onion seeds (optional)
5ml/1 tsp ground turmeric
5ml/1 tsp ground cumin
5ml/1 tsp ground coriander
5ml/1 tsp fennel seeds
salt and black pepper
a good squeeze of lemon juice
chopped fresh coriander and lemon wedges, to garnish

1 Bring a pan of salted water to the boil, add the potatoes and simmer for about 4 minutes, until just tender. Drain well.

2 Heat the oil in a large frying pan and add the garlic along with all the whole and ground spices. Fry gently for 1–2 minutes, stirring until the mustard seeds start to pop.

3 Add the potatoes and stir-fry on a moderate heat for about 5 minutes, until heated through and well coated with the spicy oil.

4 Season well and sprinkle over the lemon juice. Garnish with chopped coriander and lemon wedges. Serve as an accompaniment to curries or other strong flavoured dishes.

Spanish Chilli Potatoes

The name of this Spanish *tapas* dish, *Patatas Bravas*, means fierce, hot potatoes. You can always reduce the amount of chilli to suit your taste.

INGREDIENTS

Serves 4

1kg/2lb new or salad potatoes
60ml/4 tbsp olive oil
1 onion, finely chopped
2 garlic cloves, crushed
15ml/1 tbsp tomato purée
200g/7oz can chopped tomatoes
15ml/1 tbsp red wine vinegar
2–3 small dried red chillies, seeded and chopped finely, or 5–10ml/1–2 tsp hot chilli powder
5ml/1 tsp paprika
salt and black pepper
fresh flat leaf parsley sprig, to garnish

1 Boil the potatoes in their skins for 10–12 minutes or until just tender. Drain well and leave to cool, then cut in half and reserve.

2 Heat the oil in a large pan and add the onions and garlic. Fry gently for 5–6 minutes, until just softened. Stir in the tomato purée, tomatoes, vinegar, chilli and paprika and simmer for about 5 minutes.

3 Add the potatoes and mix into the sauce mixture until well coated. Cover and simmer gently for about 8–10 minutes, or until the potatoes are tender. Season well and transfer to a warmed serving dish. Serve garnished with a sprig of flat leaf parsley.

Bulgur Wheat Salad with Oranges and Almonds

INGREDIENTS

Serves 4

1 small green pepper
150g/5oz/1 cup bulgur wheat
600ml/1 pint/2½ cups water
¼ cucumber, diced
15g/½oz/½ cup chopped fresh mint
40g/1½oz/¾ cup flaked
  almonds, toasted
grated rind and juice of 1 lemon
2 seedless oranges
salt and black pepper
mint sprigs, to garnish

1 Using a sharp vegetable knife, carefully halve the green pepper. Discard the core and seeds, then cut the pepper into small cubes and set aside.

2 Place the bulgur wheat in a saucepan and add the water. Bring to the boil, lower the heat, cover and simmer for 10–15 minutes until tender. Alternatively, place the bulgur wheat in a heatproof bowl, pour over boiling water and leave to soak for 30 minutes. Most, if not all, of the water should be absorbed; drain off any excess.

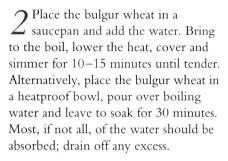

3 Toss the bulgur wheat with the cucumber, green pepper, mint and toasted almonds in a serving bowl. Add the grated lemon rind and juice.

4 Cut the rind from the oranges, then working over the bowl to catch the juice, cut the oranges into neat segments. Add to the bulgur mixture, with seasoning, and toss lightly. Garnish with the mint sprigs.

Fruity Brown Rice Salad

An Asian-style dressing gives this colourful rice salad extra piquancy. Whole grains like brown rice are unrefined, so they retain their natural fibre, vitamins and minerals.

INGREDIENTS

Serves 4–6

115g/4oz/³/₄ cup brown rice
1 small red pepper, seeded and diced
200g/7oz can sweetcorn, drained
45ml/3 tbsp sultanas
225g/8oz can pineapple pieces in fruit juice
15ml/1 tbsp light soy sauce
15ml/1 tbsp sunflower oil
15ml/1 tbsp hazelnut oil
1 garlic clove, crushed
5ml/1 tsp finely chopped fresh root ginger
salt and black pepper
4 spring onions, sliced, to garnish

1 Cook the brown rice in a large saucepan of lightly salted boiling water for about 30 minutes, or until it is tender. Drain thoroughly and cool.

2 Tip the rice into a bowl and add the red pepper, sweetcorn and sultanas. Drain the pineapple pieces, reserving the juice, add them to the rice mixture and toss lightly.

3 Pour the reserved pineapple juice into a clean screw-top jar. Add the soy sauce, sunflower and hazelnut oils, garlic and root ginger. Add some salt and pepper. Then close the jar tightly and shake well to combine.

4 Pour the dressing over the salad and toss well. Scatter the spring onions over the top. The salad is delicious as part of a summer buffet or served with grilled meat or fish.

VARIATION

Try a mixture of brown rice and wild rice instead of just the brown rice. Cook the rice mixture for the recommended time.

Egg and Tomato Salad with Crab

INGREDIENTS

Serves 4

1 round lettuce
2 x 200g/7oz cans crabmeat, drained
4 hard-boiled eggs, sliced
16 cherry tomatoes, halved
½ green pepper, seeded and
   thinly sliced
6 stoned black olives, sliced

For the dressing

250ml/8fl oz/1 cup mayonnaise
10ml/2 tsp fresh lemon juice
45ml/3 tbsp chilli sauce
½ green pepper, seeded and finely
   chopped
5ml/1 tsp prepared horseradish
5ml/1 tsp Worcestershire sauce

1 To make the dressing, place all the ingredients in a bowl and mix well. Set aside in a cool place.

2 Line four plates with the lettuce leaves. Mound the crabmeat in the centre. Arrange the eggs around the outside with the tomatoes on top.

3 Spoon some of the dressing over the crabmeat. Arrange the green pepper slices on top and sprinkle with the olives. Serve immediately with the remaining dressing.

Summer Tuna Salad

This colourful salad is perfect for a summer lunch in the garden – use canned or freshly cooked salmon in place of the tuna, if you like.

INGREDIENTS

Serves 4–6

175g/6oz radishes
1 cucumber
3 celery sticks
1 yellow pepper
175g/6oz cherry tomatoes, halved
4 spring onions, thinly sliced
45ml/3 tbsp fresh lemon juice
45ml/3 tbsp olive oil
2 x 200g/7oz cans tuna, drained and
   flaked
30ml/2 tbsp chopped fresh parsley
salt and black pepper
lettuce leaves, to serve
thin strips twisted lemon rind,
   to garnish

1 Cut the radishes, cucumber, celery and yellow pepper into small cubes. Place in a large, shallow dish with the cherry tomatoes and spring onions.

2 In a small bowl, stir together the salt and lemon juice with a fork until dissolved. Pour this over the vegetable mixture. Add the oil and pepper to taste. Stir to coat the vegetables. Cover and set aside for 1 hour.

3 Add the flaked tuna and parsley to the mixture and toss gently until well combined.

4 Arrange the lettuce leaves on a platter and spoon the salad into the centre. Garnish with the lemon rind.

VARIATION

Prepare the vegetables as above and add the parsley. Arrange lettuce leaves on individual plates and divide the vegetable mixture among them. Place a mound of tuna on top of each and finish with a dollop of mayonnaise.

DESSERTS, PUDDINGS AND CAKES

Desserts may not be served up at every meal these days, but a special meal such as Sunday lunch or when entertaining deserves that extra bit of effort. There is something for everyone and each occasion in this chapter, from summery fruit salads to warming pies and tarts, and from delicious homemade ice creams to dessert cakes, including Apple and Cinnamon Crumble Cake and Chocolate Chestnut Roulade.

Mandarin and Orange Flower Salad

Mandarins, tangerines, clementines, mineolas: any of these lovely citrus fruits are suitable for this recipe.

INGREDIENTS

Serves 4

10 mandarins
15ml/1 tbsp icing sugar
10ml/2 tsp orange flower water
15ml/1 tbsp chopped pistachio nuts

1 Thinly pare a little of the rind from one mandarin and cut it into fine shreds for decoration. Squeeze the juice from two mandarins and reserve it.

2 Peel the remaining fruit, removing as much of the white pith as possible. Arrange the whole fruit in a wide dish.

3 Mix together the reserved mandarin juice, icing sugar and orange flower water, then pour it over the fruit. Cover the dish and chill for at least 1 hour.

4 Blanch the shreds of mandarin rind in boiling water for 30 seconds. Drain, then leave to cool before sprinkling them over the mandarins, with the pistachio nuts.

Fruit Compote

Some of the best fruit salads are a mixture of fresh and dried fruits. This salad features some of the most delicious summer and winter fruits available, but you could experiment with almost any fruit – they combine together beautifully.

INGREDIENTS

Serves 4
115g/4oz dried apricots
115g/4oz dried peaches
115g/4oz prunes
2 oranges, peeled and sliced

For the syrup
1 lemon
4 green cardamom pods
1 cinnamon stick
150ml/¼ pint/ ¾ cup clear honey
30ml/2 tbsp ginger syrup from the jar
3 pieces stem ginger

1 Soak the apricots, peaches and prunes in enough cold water to cover, for 1–2 hours until they have plumped up.

2 Meanwhile, make the syrup: pare two strips of rind from the lemon with a potato peeler or sharp knife. Halve the lemon and squeeze the juice from one half.

3 Lightly crush the cardamom pods with the back of a large, heavy-bladed knife.

4 Place the lemon rind, cardamom, cinnamon stick, honey, ginger syrup and lemon juice in a heavy-based saucepan. Add 60ml/4 tbsp water, bring to the boil and simmer for 2 minutes. Set aside while making the fruit compote.

5 Drain the apricots, peaches and prunes and cut in half, or quarters if large. Place in a large pan with the oranges. Add 475ml/16fl oz/2 cups water, bring to the boil and simmer for 10 minutes until the fruit is tender.

6 Add the honey and ginger syrup, stir well and simmer for a further 1–2 minutes. Allow the compote to cool, then chill it in the fridge for about 1–2 hours or overnight.

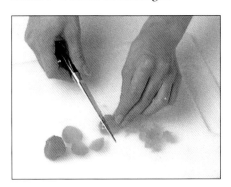

7 Chop the pieces of stem ginger and sprinkle them over the compote just before serving.

Emerald Fruit Salad

The cool, green coloured fruits make a refreshing mixture in this delicious fruit salad.

INGREDIENTS

Serves 4
30ml/2 tbsp lime juice
30ml/2 tbsp clear honey
2 green eating apples, cored and sliced
1 small ripe melon, diced
2 kiwi fruit, sliced
1 star fruit, sliced
mint sprigs, to decorate
yogurt or fromage frais, to serve

1 Mix together the lime juice and honey in a large bowl, then toss the apple slices in this.

2 Stir in the melon, kiwi fruit and star fruit. Place in a glass serving dish and chill.

3 Decorate the fruit salad with mint sprigs and serve with yogurt or fromage frais.

VARIATION

Add other green fruits when available, such as greengages, grapes, pears or kiwano, which is a type of melon. It has a tough yellowy orange rind covered with sharp spikes, and the flesh inside looks like a bright green jelly, encasing edible seeds which can be removed with a spoon.

Coconut Ice Cream

An easy-to-make, quite heavenly, ice cream that will be loved by all for its tropical taste.

INGREDIENTS

Serves 8

400g/14oz can evaporated milk
400g/14oz can condensed milk
400g/14oz can coconut milk
freshly grated nutmeg
5ml/1 tsp almond essence
lemon balm sprigs, lime slices and
  shredded coconut, to decorate

1 Mix together the evaporated, condensed and coconut milks in a large freezerproof bowl and stir in the nutmeg and almond essence.

2 Chill in a freezer for an hour or two until the mixture is semi-frozen.

3 Remove from the freezer and whisk the mixture with a hand or electric whisk until it is fluffy and almost doubled in volume.

4 Pour into a freezer container, then cover and freeze. Soften slightly before serving, decorated with lemon balm, lime slices and shredded coconut.

Apple Froth

This is another very popular dessert. It is easy to make and is perfect after a rich meal.

INGREDIENTS

Serves 4
4 apples
30ml/2 tbsp lemon juice
30ml/2 tbsp rose-water
45–60ml/3–4 tbsp icing sugar
crushed ice, to serve

--- COOK'S TIP ---

Pears are also excellent in this light refreshing dessert. Choose ripe pears if using them. They will yield when gently pressed at the stalk end, but take care not to bruise them.

1 Carefully and thinly cut the peel from the apples using a swivel peeler. Discard the peel. Work quickly, otherwise the apples will begin to brown. If necessary, place the peeled apples in a bowl of lemony water while you peel the others.

2 Grate the apples coarsely into a bowl, discarding the cores, then transfer to a pretty serving dish.

3 Stir in the lemon juice, rose-water and add icing sugar to taste.

4 Chill for at least 30 minutes and serve with crushed ice.

Pineapple Ice Cream

INGREDIENTS

Serves 8–10
8 eggs, separated
115g/4oz/½ cup caster sugar
2.5ml/½ tsp vanilla essence
600ml/1 pint/2½ cups whipping cream
60ml/4 tbsp icing sugar
425g/15oz can pineapple chunks
75g/3oz/¾ cup pistachio nuts, chopped
wafer biscuits, to serve

1 Place the egg yolks in a bowl, add the sugar and vanilla essence and beat until thick and pale.

2 In a separate bowl, whip the cream and icing sugar to soft peaks, add to the egg yolk mixture and mix well.

3 Whisk the egg whites in a separate large bowl until they are firm and hold stiff peaks. Gently fold the egg whites into the cream mixture and blend well.

4 Cut the pineapple into very small pieces, add the pistachio nuts and stir into the cream mixture and mix well with a spoon.

5 Pour the mixture into an ice cream container and place in the freezer for a few hours until it is set and firm, stirring it once or twice.

6 Cut into thick slices and serve in a pretty glass dish decorated with wafer biscuits.

Rhubarb Pie

INGREDIENTS

Serves 6

175g/6oz/1½ cups plain flour
2.5ml/½ tsp salt
10ml/2 tsp caster sugar
75g/3oz/6 tbsp cold butter or mar-
    garine
50ml/2fl oz/¼ cup or more iced water
30ml/2 tbsp single cream

For the filling

1kg/2lb fresh rhubarb, cut into
    2.5cm/1in slices
30ml/2 tbsp cornflour
1 egg
275g/10oz/1½ cups caster sugar
15ml/1 tbsp grated orange rind

1 To make the pastry, sift the flour, salt and sugar into a bowl. Using a pastry blender or two knives, cut the butter or margarine into the dry ingredients as quickly as possible until the mixture resembles breadcrumbs.

2 Sprinkle the flour mixture with the iced water and mix until the dough just holds together. If the dough is too crumbly, add a little more water, 15ml/1 tbsp at a time.

COOK'S TIP

Use milk in place of the single cream to glaze the pie, if you prefer. Or for a crisp crust, brush the pastry with water and sprinkle with caster sugar instead.

3 Gather the dough into a ball, flatten into a round, place in a polythene bag and chill for 20 minutes.

4 Roll out the pastry between two sheets of greaseproof paper to a 3mm/⅛in thickness. Use to line a 23cm/9in pie dish or tin. Trim all around, leaving a 1cm/½in overhang. Fold the overhang under the edge and flute. Chill the pastry case and trimmings for at least 30 minutes.

5 To make the filling, put the rhubarb in a bowl, sprinkle with the cornflour and toss to coat.

6 Preheat the oven to 220°C/425°F/ Gas 7. Beat the egg with the sugar in a bowl until thoroughly blended, then mix in the orange rind.

7 Stir the sugar mixture into the rhubarb and mix well, then spoon the fruit into the pastry case.

8 Roll out the pastry trimmings. Stamp out decorative shapes with a biscuit cutter or cut shapes with a small knife, using a cardboard template as a guide, if your prefer.

9 Arrange the pastry shapes on top of the pie. Brush the shapes and the edge of the pastry case with cream.

10 Bake the pie for 30 minutes. Reduce the oven temperature to 160°C/325°F/Gas 3 and continue baking for a further 15–20 minutes, until the pastry is golden brown and the rhubarb is tender. Serve the pie hot with cream.

Pear and Blueberry Pie

INGREDIENTS

Serves 4

225g/8oz/2 cups plain flour
pinch of salt
50g/2oz/4 tbsp lard, cubed
50g/2oz/4 tbsp butter, cubed
675g/1½lb blueberries
30ml/2 tbsp caster sugar
15ml/1 tbsp arrowroot
2 ripe, but firm pears, peeled, cored
  and sliced
2.5ml/½ tsp ground cinnamon
grated rind of ½ lemon
beaten egg white, to glaze
caster sugar, for sprinkling
crème fraîche, to serve

1 Sift the flour and salt into a bowl and rub in the lard and butter until the mixture resembles fine breadcrumbs. Stir in 45ml/3 tbsp cold water and mix to a dough. Chill for 30 minutes.

2 Place 225g/8oz of the blueberries in a pan with the sugar. Cover and cook gently until the blueberries have softened. Press through a nylon sieve.

3 Blend the arrowroot with 30ml/ 2 tbsp cold water and add to the blueberry purée. Bring to the boil, stirring until thickened. Cool slightly.

4 Place a baking sheet in the oven and preheat to 190°C/375°F/Gas 5. Roll out just over half the pastry on a lightly floured surface and use to line a 20cm/8in shallow pie dish or plate.

5 Mix together the remaining blueberries, the pears, cinnamon and lemon rind and spoon into the dish. Pour over the blueberry purée.

6 Roll out the remaining pastry and use to cover the pie. Make a small slit in the centre. Brush with egg white and sprinkle with caster sugar. Bake the pie on the hot baking sheet, for 40–45 minutes, until golden. Serve warm with crème fraîche.

Almond Syrup Tart

INGREDIENTS

Serves 6

75g/3oz fresh white breadcrumbs
225g/8oz golden syrup
finely grated rind of ½ lemon
10ml/2 tsp lemon juice
23cm/9in shortcrust pastry case
25g/1oz flaked almonds

1 Preheat the oven to 200°C/400°F/ Gas 6. In a mixing bowl, combine the breadcrumbs with the golden syrup and the lemon rind and juice.

2 Spoon into the pastry case and spread out evenly.

3 Sprinkle the flaked almonds evenly over the top.

4 Brush the pastry with milk to glaze, if you like. Bake for 25–30 minutes or until the pastry and filling are golden brown.

5 Remove to a wire rack to cool. Serve warm or cold, with cream, custard or ice cream.

COOK'S TIP

For Walnut Syrup Tart, replace the almonds with chopped walnuts. For Ginger Syrup Tart, mix 5ml/1 tsp ground ginger with the breadcrumbs before adding the syrup and lemon rind and juice. Omit the nuts if liked. For Coconut Syrup Tart, replace 25g/1oz of the bread-crumbs with 40g/1½oz of desiccated coconut.

Peanut Butter Tart

INGREDIENTS

Serves 8

175g/6oz digestive biscuits, crushed
50g/2oz/¼ cup soft light brown sugar
75g/3oz/6 tbsp butter or margarine,
  melted
whipped cream or ice cream, to serve

For the filling

3 egg yolks
90g/3½oz/½ cup caster sugar
50g/2oz/¼ cup soft light brown sugar
25g/1oz/¼ cup cornflour
600ml/1 pint/2½ cups canned
  evaporated milk
25g/1oz/2 tbsp unsalted butter or
  margarine
7.5ml/1½ tsp vanilla essence
115g/4oz crunchy peanut butter
75g/3oz/¾ cup icing sugar

1 Preheat the oven to 180°C/350°F/
Gas 4. Grease a 23cm/9in pie dish.

2 Mix together the biscuit crumbs,
sugar and butter or margarine in a
bowl and blend well. Spread the mixture in the prepared dish, pressing the
mixture evenly over the base and sides
with your fingertips.

3 Bake the crumb crust for 10 minutes. Remove from the oven and
leave to cool. Leave the oven on.

4 To make the filling, mix together
the egg yolks, caster and brown
sugars and cornflour in a heavy-based
saucepan using a wooden spoon,

5 Slowly whisk in the milk, then
cook over a medium heat for about
8–10 minutes, stirring constantly, until
the mixture thickens. Reduce the heat
to very low and cook for a further 3–4
minutes, until the mixture is very thick.

6 Beat in the butter or margarine
and the vanilla essence. Remove
the pan from the heat, then cover the
surface loosely with clear film and cool.

> ——— COOK'S TIP ———
> If preferred, use an equal amount of finely
> crushed ginger snaps in place of digestive
> biscuits for the crumb crust. Or make the
> pie with a ready-made pastry case.

7 Combine the peanut butter with
the icing sugar in a small bowl,
working with your fingertips to blend
the ingredients to the consistency of
fine breadcrumbs.

8 Sprinkle all but 45ml/3 tbsp of the
peanut butter crumbs evenly over
the base of the crumb crust.

9 Pour in the filling, spreading it
into an even layer, then sprinkle
with the remaining crumbs and bake
for 15 minutes. Leave the pie to cool
for at least 1 hour. Serve with whipped
cream or ice cream.

Bread and Butter Custard

This dessert is a delicious family favourite. A richer version can be made with fresh cream, instead of evaporated milk. It can also be made using other dried fruit – mango is particularly good.

INGREDIENTS

Serves 4

15ml/1 tbsp softened butter
3 thin slices of bread, crusts removed
400g/14oz can evaporated milk
150ml/¼ pint/⅔ cup fresh milk
2.5ml/½ tsp mixed spice
40g/1½oz/3 tbsp demerara sugar
2 eggs, whisked
75g/3oz/½ cup sultanas
freshly grated nutmeg
a little icing sugar, for dusting

1 Preheat the oven to 180°C/350°F/ Gas 4 and lightly butter an ovenproof dish. Butter the bread and cut into small pieces.

2 Lay the buttered bread in several layers in the prepared dish.

3 Whisk together the evaporated milk and the fresh milk, mixed spice, sugar and eggs in a large bowl. Pour the mixture over the bread and butter. Sprinkle over the sultanas and leave to stand for 30 minutes.

4 Grate a little nutmeg over the top and bake for 30–40 minutes until the custard is just set and golden. Serve sprinkled with icing sugar.

Warm Lemon and Syrup Cake

INGREDIENTS

Serves 8

3 eggs
175g/6oz/¾ cup butter, softened
175g/6oz/¾ cup caster sugar
175g/6oz/1½ cups self-raising flour
50g/2oz/½ cup ground almonds
1.25ml/¼ tsp freshly grated nutmeg
50g/2oz candied lemon peel,
   finely chopped
grated rind of 1 lemon
30ml/2 tbsp lemon juice
poached pears, to serve

For the syrup

175g/6oz/¾ cup caster sugar
juice of 3 lemons

1 Preheat the oven to 180°C/350°F/
Gas 4. Grease and base-line a deep,
round 20cm/8in cake tin.

2 Place all the cake ingredients in a
large bowl and beat well for 2–3
minutes, until light and fluffy.

3 Tip the mixture into the prepared
tin, spread level and bake for 1 hour,
or until golden and firm to the touch.

4 Meanwhile, make the syrup. Put
the sugar, lemon juice and 75ml/5
tbsp water in a pan. Heat gently, stirring
until the sugar has dissolved, then boil,
without stirring, for 1–2 minutes.

5 Turn out the cake on to a plate with
a rim. Prick the surface of the cake
all over with a fork, then pour over the
hot syrup. Leave to soak for about 30
minutes. Serve the cake warm with thin
wedges of poached pears.

Apple and Cinnamon Crumble Cake

This scrumptious cake has layers of spicy fruit and crumble and is quite delicious served warm with fresh cream.

INGREDIENTS

Makes 1 cake
3 large cooking apples
2.5ml/½ tsp ground cinnamon
250g/9oz/1 cup butter
250g/9oz/1¼ cups caster sugar
4 eggs
450g/1lb/4 cups self-raising flour

For the crumble topping
175g/6oz/¾ cup demerara sugar
125g/4¼oz/1¼ cups plain flour
5ml/1 tsp ground cinnamon
65g/2½oz/about 4½ tbsp desiccated coconut
115g/4oz/½ cup butter

1 Preheat the oven to 180°C/350°F/ Gas 4. Grease a 25cm/10in round cake tin and line the base with greaseproof paper. To make the crumble topping, mix together the sugar, flour, cinnamon and coconut in a bowl, then rub in the butter with your fingertips and set aside.

2 Peel and core the apples, then grate them coarsely. Place them in a bowl, sprinkle with the cinnamon and set aside.

3 Cream the butter and sugar in a bowl with an electric mixer, until light and fluffy. Beat in the eggs, one at a time, beating well after each addition.

4 Sift in half the flour, mix well, then add the remaining flour and stir until smooth.

5 Spread half the cake mixture evenly over the base of the prepared tin. Spoon the apples on top and scatter over half the crumble topping.

6 Spread the remaining cake mixture over the crumble and finally top with the remaining crumble topping.

7 Bake for 1 hour 10 minutes – 1 hour 20 minutes, covering the cake with foil if it browns too quickly. Leave in the tin for about 5 minutes, before turning out on to a wire rack. Once cool, cut into slices to serve.

COOK'S TIP

To make the topping in a food processor, add all the ingredients and process for a few seconds until the mixture resembles breadcrumbs. You can also grate the apples using the grating disc. If you don't have a 25cm/10in round tin you can use a 20cm/8in square cake tin.

Chocolate Chestnut Roulade

This moist chocolate sponge has a soft, mousse-like texture as it contains no flour. Don't worry if it cracks as you roll it up – this is typical of a good roulade.

INGREDIENTS

Serves 8
175g/6oz plain chocolate
30ml/2 tbsp strong black coffee
5 eggs, separated
175g/6oz/¾ cup caster sugar
250ml/8fl oz/1 cup double cream
225g/8oz unsweetened chestnut
  purée
45–60ml/3–4 tbsp icing sugar, plus
  extra for dusting
single cream, to serve

1 Preheat the oven to 180°C/350°F/ Gas 4. Line a 33 x 23cm/13 x 9in Swiss roll tin with non-stick baking paper and brush lightly with oil.

2 Break up the chocolate into a bowl and set over a pan of barely simmering water. Allow the chocolate to melt, then stir until smooth. Remove the bowl from the pan and stir in the coffee. Leave to cool slightly.

3 Whisk the egg yolks and sugar together in a separate bowl, until thick and light, then stir in the cooled chocolate mixture.

4 Whisk the egg whites in another bowl until they hold stiff peaks. Stir a spoonful into the chocolate mixture to lighten it, then gently fold in the rest.

5 Pour the mixture into the prepared tin, and gently spread level. Bake for 20 minutes. Remove the roulade from the oven, then cover the cooked roulade with a clean dish towel and leave to cool in the tin for several hours, or preferably overnight.

6 Whip the cream until it forms soft peaks. Mix together the chestnut purée and icing sugar until smooth, then fold into the whipped cream.

7 Lay a piece of greaseproof paper on the work surface and dust with icing sugar. Turn out the roulade on to the paper and carefully peel off the lining paper. Trim the sides.

8 Gently spread the chestnut cream evenly over the roulade to within 2.5cm/1in of the edges.

9 Using the greaseproof paper to help you, carefully roll up the roulade as tightly and evenly as possible.

10 Chill the roulade for about 2 hours, then sprinkle liberally with icing sugar. Cut into thick slices and serve with a little single cream poured over each slice.

COOK'S TIP

Make sure that you whisk the egg yolks and sugar for at least 5 minutes to incorporate as much air as possible.

Index